IF ONLY...

THE DECLINE AND FALL OF ENGLAND AS A FOOTBALL SUPERPOWER

First published 2014 by DB Publishing, an imprint of JMD Media Ltd, Nottingham, United Kingdom.

ISBN 9781780913643

IF ONLY...

THE DECLINE AND FALL OF ENGLAND AS A FOOTBALL SUPERPOWER

CHRIS SHEPPARDSON

Dedicated to Imogen and Francesca

"Football is a simple game based on the giving and taking of passes, of controlling the ball and of making yourself available to receive a pass. It is terribly simple."[1]

Bill Shankly.

1   Bill Shankly. (2014) *Own Words*. [Online] Available from: http://www.shankly.com/article/2517 [Accessed: 21 October 2014].

Contents

The Night Reality Dawned

17 October 1973 – England 1 Poland 1.

England had failed to qualify for the
1974 World Cup Finals in West Germany.

"If the game had been a boxing match, it would have been
stopped as it was so one sided. In fact England would have
won on points even if it had been. Football can be so cruel."
Martin (supporter) on England v Poland 1973.[2]

England's failure to qualify for the 1974 World Cup Finals was a
shock to most in the country. In 1970, England possessed a team
still able to play at the highest level of competitive International football and just three years later, England had failed to qualify. It had
become clear after the 1972 European Nations Cup defeat to West
Germany that the players from the 1966 triumph were closing in on
the end of their days but the belief was that England had strength
in-depth and that England would still be a top eight team come
the 74 finals. That belief came to a silent end as Poland qualified at
England's expense.

The initial reaction was that England had simply been unlucky, as
the Polish goalkeeper had made a string of excellent saves. It was also
thought that it was all individual player error that had cost England
dear – Norman Hunter missed a crucial tackle and Peter Shilton did
not seem to react quickly enough on the Polish goal – but, all this
missed the fact that England's Captain, the great Martin Peters had
been forced to resort to diving to win a penalty to find a way back

---

    Focus group – London, February 2014.

into the game. England had not played well during the whole qualifying group and the result of that October evening simply marked a fair fate for a country and team that had lost its way.

If one looks back at International Football in the 1970s, it is clear that England simply neither evolved their thinking from the success they had found under Ramsey nor did they heed the lessons of what was taking place on the International scene. Maybe it is an English curse as the same happened with both the England rugby team after their 2003 triumph and the England cricket team after they reached the No.1 side status. Sport evolves and does not stop still. For many reasons, England did not evolve as others had in Europe post 1968.

Ramsey achieved success through creating a winning formula that combined a number of great players within a system that played to their strengths. Ramsey's system brought the best out of Bobby Charlton who could run, with menace, at the opposition from midfield and make them defensive in their mind-set, conscious of his threat. Peters could "ghost" into positions to score goals and play the telling pass. Ball added energy and guile whilst Banks and Moore were simply giants in their positions, able to repel attackers. Ramsey's success relied on the combination of great organization and a core of world-class players. Once this core broke down – as was seen against West Germany in both 1970 and in 1972 – then England were vulnerable. England believed that they had one of the best teams in the world but the truth was that it relied on a few great players. This lasted till 1970 but after the Mexico World Cup, the players began to fade and England's troubles began in earnest. 1973 was not even the low point. Arguably that would come in 1976 and 1977 as England failed to qualify for the 1978 World Cup and England's manager, Don Revie, resigned to take the offerings of financial wealth in the Middle East. Rightly or wrongly, England felt betrayed.

Of course, there was more depth to the problems that were to come. England still possessed a range of potentially exceptional players waiting in the wings to learn how to play at the highest level. Ramsey though continued with his tried and tested formula whilst other teams evolved their approach, thinking and adding technical play to break down well-organised sides. The English club teams of the early 1970s all followed Ramsey's lead and the nearly all teams in the First and Second Divisions were all well organised, compact and very competitive. It is no coincidence that Second Division teams enjoyed their greatest success in the FA Cup from 72–80 with three victories and a further finalist.

The game in the early years of the 1970s did not encourage players with skill and flair that wanted to be attack minded. Defence was the foundation stone on which winning teams were built.

However, Brazil had won the World Cup in 1970 with thrilling play that made the game appear beautiful. Yes, England competed effectively with Brazil and they could – and maybe should have drawn 1–1. However, that would have been a successful result for England whilst Brazil could have beaten England 2–0. Brazil respected England and played the game accordingly. Against other sides, their attacking play inspired children all across the world to play the game with panache. Already teams were working out that a well-organised team was vulnerable against excellent ball players that could do the inspired. Brazil led the way and this was followed by both Holland and West Germany in 1974. Both teams were well organised and had attacking philosophies.

If one can sit back objectively and imagine how the England team that played Poland in 1973 would have fared against the Holland side of Cruyff and Neeskens, then in truth England was still a step behind. Ramsey's fresh new team of 73 could have grown into an excellent

International team with Tony Currie, Martin Chivers, Colin Bell, Peter Shilton and Roy McFarland as its core but they were simply not ready for the immediate challenge. They lacked experience, the "learning" and guile needed for the highest level. It generally takes 3–4 years for a team, to evolve to be world class. The 73 England team was being built for the 74 finals in less than two years and it showed.

Ramsey maybe realised too late that the game had evolved and he needed to change. In fairness to the great man, he did change and was building a new team but it was just a year too late. Given another year and England could have fielded a team that were quarter-finalists. England had the calibre of player and quality to compete to a good level in 74 and in 78, but the English obsession with defence and systems undermined the need for developing International flair players that could unlock defences.

Make no mistake; England possessed the depth and quality of player that could have been developed into very good International players but for many reasons never quite made it beyond a certain level. Consider Tony Currie, Martin Chivers, Gerry Francis, Colin Todd, Roy McFarland, David Nish, Alan Hudson, Allan Clarke, Ray Kennedy, Keith Weller, Frank Worthington, Billy Bonds, Graham Paddon and even Jimmy Case. Jimmy Case never played for England – in fact. He was the only Liverpool player that won the 77 European Cup that was not an International and yet was competing at the top of European competition. Of all the others, most won less than 20 caps for England.

Joe Mercer, in his short period of time as Caretaker Manager (1974), managed to find a balance between defence and attacking flair that had England playing competitive football again. Many commented that England played some of their best football since 1970 under Mercer. It arguably needed a man that was one step removed from the rivalry of club football and maybe Mercer would have been the right man to succeed Ramsey, as he appeared to understand what was needed and more importantly, understood players. He had the ability to bring them together as a united team in a short period of time. Revie never won over the players and as time wore on, Revie's teams became increasingly negative in their play. Mercer could relate to the players. He stood above club football and the players responded.

Ron Greenwood was similar – he was the architect of the great West Ham team of the 1960s with Moore, Hurst and Peters. He too had moved away from club football. The intense rivalries that existed in club football created an underlying tension that was difficult for Revie to overcome and eventually undermined him. It was to be Greenwood that would gradually nurse England back to health through finding a balance that encouraged attacking play that could unlock the best defences in the world game.

Historically England's attacking prowess lay in a combination of a strong physical centre-forward combined with wingers that would attack the full-backs and send in cross after cross to threaten the opposition's goal. Stanley Mathews and Ton Finney allowed the England teams of the late 30s and 40s really compete effectively.

Ramsey had built a system – the wingless wonders – that worked for a period of time and won England the World Cup. It worked until the core of his team faded in their powers and superior teams developed strategies to reduce the threat. England had become too predictable and their play lacked inspiration and flair.

Greenwood's team of the late 70s possessed a balance that had the physical presence of a strong centre forward – Bob Latchford – served by two wingers and supported with the subtle runs and skill of Trevor Brooking ad Kevin Keegan who was the fulcrum of the team.

Suddenly England looked balanced and possessed more variety to their play.

If one analyses what are arguably England's two best teams since 1970 in 1990 and 1996, one can see the skill and balance to both attack and defend. In 1996, under Terry Venables, England had again the strong physical presence of a traditional English centre-forward in Alan Shearer supported alongside him by the subtle approach play of Terry Sheringham and supported by Steve McManaman and Darren Anderton – both with the ability to unlock a defensive system with a moment of skill – supported by Paul Gascoigne. In defence, England were resolute with David Seaman (Goalkeeper), Tony Adams, Stuart Pearce, Gary Neville, Gareth Southgate and Paul Ince in a holding position. Arguably this was England's most exciting and balanced team since the great days as World Champions and England played some superb football – most especially against Holland who England destroyed 4–1 in the 1996 European Championships.

The 1990 team, under Bobby Robson, also possessed a similar structure with the able Gary Lineker supported by Peter Beardsley and by two more excellent wingers in John Barnes and Chris Waddle. Paul Gascoigne played some of his best football as the attacking threat from midfield and David Platt came into the team to score some very important goals with late runs into the box. Again, this line up possessed both balance and the unpredictable that could unlock the very best defences. In the rearguard, stood a defence that included Shilton, Terry Butcher, Stuart Pearce, and Paul Parker. In the semi-final against Germany, England matched Germany in every aspect of the game, bar the skill to take penalties under pressure.

It is easy to see why both these England teams had their golden moments when the team came together as a genuinely competitive force. In the 1986 World Cup, England scared Argentina as John

Barnes ran at them and could, with luck, have drawn level after trailing 2–0. England's history has been built around a mix of strong physical players combined with players that would run at the opposition and carry threat and menace – Stanley Matthews, Tom Finney, Bobby Charlton, John Barnes, Peter Barnes, Darren Anderton, Steve McManaman and Chris Waddle. English crowds have always loved and risen to great wing play as also shown by Ryan Giggs, George Best, Christano Ronaldo, Mike Summerbee, Steve Heighway, Charlie Cooke, and Eddie Gray, to name just a few that played in the league over the years.

It serves to highlight the lack of creativity and flair that existed within the systems that so dominated the 70s. England simply defeated themselves by employing tactics and strategies that were successful but became outdated quickly. The world game had moved on and England had fallen behind.

"Football is all about emotion. That is what sucks you in. You live for those moments when your team triumphs after all the pain. With England it just takes twice as long."

Dick (Supporter).[3]

Introduction

17 October 1973 – England v Poland at Wembley Stadium.

As England walked out onto the Wembley turf, they needed to win their final World Cup qualification match against a traditionally under achieving team to qualify for the World Cup Finals. England had been World Champions in 1966 and arguably had their best ever team in 1970. That was just three years ago and surely they had not declined so much that they could not qualify?

Time had, though, run out on England as they drew the match 1–1. The result shocked the nation and began a period of exile from major International competition that was to last until 1980. Six years may not seem a long time but England possessed players that were able to compete with the very best. The significance of the 1973 result was that it highlighted that the infrastructure of the game and the mind-set that dominated the club scene was not just preparing the ground for success on the world stage. Failure had been coming for some time and change was needed but would still take many more years, and no little heartache, before it took place.

England – fans, players, the game's administrators – had believed their own PR for too long because England's club teams were a competitive force in European competition. However, in the International arena, England had been struggling to win important matches for a long period running back to even pre-1970 World Cup.

In 1970, England were one of the pre-tournament favourites mainly based on the calibre of the world class players that sat within their ranks – Bobby Moore, Bobby Charlton, Gordon Banks, Alan Ball, Martin Peters and Geoff Hurst. They were some of England's greatest players to have ever taken the field but from after the 1968

European Nations Cup semi-final defeat, England had struggled to be competitive at the highest levels.

If one is coldly objective, England's results justified only their reaching only the quarter-final in 1970. Results leading up to the match suggested that England were vulnerable against the best attacking teams. The signs were there for all to see but few, if any, had recognised them and the loss was explained away by individual error. It was only the 1972 defeat to West Germany, which many identified as the match that illustrated England were a team past its sell by date. Success relied on a few players and there was no real depth of class players able to play against the very best on the International stage. International sport is about depth of talent and squads and England did not possess a squad with the depth to maintain the success of the mid-60s.

If one wants to understand England's struggles in the 1970s, then one needs to look back to its moment of triumph in 66. Similarly, the road to success in 1966 had started in the mid-1950s as the club game began to nurture world-class talent again for the first time since the Second World War – talent led by the likes of Duncan Edwards and Johnny Haynes. It took over 10 years to achieve success in 66 and the decline that became apparent in 1972 has started in the late 60s as the club game was led and dominated not by World Class players but by club icons. Of the top English teams in the 70s, few were captained by England's finest bar West Ham, which was a middle table team. The club game was led and dominated by a new breed of hard man that led a defensive revolution against the flair players that excited the crowds throughout the decades. The early 70s saw players such Tommy Smith, Ron Harris, Billy Bremner, Dave Mackay, Frank McLintock, and Tony Book become the leading Captains. These were tough, uncompromising players that would never give an inch and lead by example to the applause of their fans. But they were not the world-class players that one would expect from a country that had pretensions of competing for a World Cup.

The irony is that the England team that took the field in October 1973 was a New England team being rebuilt. It had real fresh talent in its ranks but it had just not had enough time to come together as a team. Ramsey had been too loyal to his players and had only begun rebuilding after even the most average fan could see the reality.

The team, if it had beaten Poland, could have grown and become a very competitive team on the World Stage. Over the next nine years that England stood in exile from the major competitions, England possessed the players to compete, so the question has to be asked as to why England struggled like they did? Why did a nation with more football teams than almost any other, with an intense passion for the game amongst players and supporters fall from grace?

This is the story of a decade that was full of contradictions, a decade where England struggled to adapt to a new modern game that was led by West Germany and Holland.

Arguably, England's victory in 66 was the start of its decline as it hid a thousand wrongs that were to follow.

As the final whistle blew at the end of the match in 1973, one could almost sense a nation's stomach churn with disappointment, as England was eliminated from the 1974 World Cup. This was to become a feeling that was to occur only too frequently over the next decade.

But that is the beauty of sport – the emotion it conjures up within you. It can bring the greatest joy to the heart stopping moments before turning to true despair. Some will say it is just a game. Very true, it is but that is hardly the point – it is passion, tribalism, patriotism, belief, and hope all rolled into one. The great Bill Shankly,

Liverpool's manager in the 60s and early 70s, once remarked: "Some people believe football is a matter of life and death, I am very disappointed with that attitude. I can assure you it is much, much more important than that." This comment reflected the passion and intensity that filled football stadiums each week and which represented how the likes of Tommy Smith, Ron Harris, Frank McLintock, and Billy Bremner approached the game and as exciting as it was for the fan, it was not a breeding ground for world class talent able to compete with the likes of Cruyff, Neeskens, Beckenbauer and Muller.

However, England still boasted a large number of excellent footballers, playing within very competitive teams. Football was an escape from everyday hardship of the economic woes that plagued the country in 73. Football was important. Leeds were seen to be ready to take on the best of Europe with one of the best teams that had ever been built in club football. Tottenham Hotspur and Wolverhampton Wanderers had battled out the UEFA Cup Final in 1972. Little known Derby County had reached the semi-finals of the European Cup in 1972. Liverpool won the UEFA Cup in 1973. England's finest clubs could compete on equal terms with the best of Europe.

So how could England have failed to qualify for the World Cup in Germany?

The club scene had become a formidable arena with a whole number of very competitive teams but there was a real battle between the technically skilful and the hard men that came to dominate the 1970s. George Best stood apart as an attacking player of skill, but he was one of a few that came into battle with the hard men of English football that the clubs and fans adored. English football became not just a match between team against team but between the flair players and hard, no nonsense tackling defenders that had become dominant both on and off the pitch. And here lies one of the crucial features of English football in the early 70s.

Tommy Smith and Ron Harris were both captains of their clubs: both were true, loyal servants to their clubs and both were adored by the fans on the terraces. Their approach to the game was whole-hearted and based on the old British premise of, "never give an inch and never shirk a tackle" and of course, many within their clubs followed their leadership and example. This meant that the English teams were united and combative in every game but that the technically skilled players were pushed aside. No one could ever doubt the spirit that lived in every team and this spirit was admired across the world – but it would not win matches alone. English football became a "blood 'n thunder" occasion that was exciting, fast and full of incident and drama. It was not an environment to nurture those of a different ilk.

This would last for a generation. Duncan McKenzie was often regarded as one of most talented players to emerge in the mid 70s but he never quite made the grade. Peter Marinello joined Arsenal in the early 70s with a great reputation but this too faded away. Glenn Hoddle emerged at Spurs in the late 70s and was widely admired and feted but never fully trusted by England. The naturally gifted were seen as a luxury to many teams. Keegan was feted as he had worked hard to make himself the best he could be. English football admired that trait but mistrusted the likes of Peter Osgood, Rodney Marsh and McKenzie who possessed technical skill. English football had arguably lost its balance. It had loved players such as Stanley Matthews and Tom Finney and in days gone by had been able to find room for both the naturally gifted plus hard workers but the balance had shifted.

English football was dominated by toughness and it could be

a very cynical game at times. It is hard to imagine a Johan Cruyff emerge in England as he did with Ajax in the 70s. Cruyff became the symbol of Total Football that caught the World game's imagination in the 74 World Cup and this illustrated the gap between the English game, mentality and that of other nations. England had become insular and was caught up in its own importance and the result was that the national team struggled to compete.

There were those that did see that the balance was all wrong. Brian Clough's famous argument with Don Revie on television after his sacking at Leeds highlighted the underlying problem. Clough had taken over from Revie as manager of Leeds United and had tried to change the culture at the club, which he saw as being cynical and not in the spirit of the game. His error was that he clearly had a burning anger at Leeds behaviour over many years and had tried to change the culture too quickly and he failed in spectacular fashion. But arguably Clough was right. Clough was more "suited" to be manager of England than Revie. Clough was the rising talent in tune with the 70s. If the FA had had the courage to appoint a man such as Clough, could history have been different?

Ramsey too could see the problem and understood that England possessed precious few players that technically stood above the club game and were world class. It is why he stayed so loyal and true to players in decline. Ramsey was no fool. He understood the World game better than anyone and knew what it took to compete but he could only work with the players that he had. If one looks at the 73 team, it was filled by players that were technically skilled and could be nurtured. In those days, very few players went and played club football abroad but if they could – as happens today – then England could have had a very good team, as the players were good enough. The English game just did not nurture International players.

After 1973, the disappointments grew more common over the following decade as England struggled with their confidence, and were not united as a team in their approach to big games. The disappointments came with increased regularity – in Czechoslovakia 1975, in Italy 1977, and there were others. Even when we did qualify for the World Cup in 1982, there were some unsettling moments along the way – defeats in Switzerland and Norway in 1981 come to the mind. To many, it still remained a mystery as to why England struggled as badly, as our club game flourished. However, the harsh truth is that if one takes away the home triumph in 1966, there is a long history where England has under-performed when it has mattered. England's club teams went from strength to strength but Internationally England under achieved.

Most football historians will talk of England's quite dramatic slide from being World Champions in 66; to possessing arguably their most complete side in 1970 to a period of failure and being in the wilderness until 1982. This is all factually true. England did underachieve for a decade, but if the result had been different on that famous October night in 1973 against Poland and England had gone to the 1974 World Cup, how different would history have been?

Why the question? For England arguably possessed their most naturally talented squad ever and if they had more time to gel as a squad and team, they could have competed against the very best in Germany 1974. Sport is so much about confidence, but confidence never grew on the international stage, as the club game was so dominant. One has to remember that the English players never had much preparation time for matches. They would come together on a Sunday evening for a Wednesday match. The players would be playing against each other in full intensity on a Saturday and then were almost expected to be team-mates three days later. Of course, it did not work, and it took a long period before this was recognised. At the same time, other nations understood the importance of rest and diet well before the English clubs. England may have had the players but the football environment that nurtured them was not one to nurture world-class players. The players that did emerge did so in spite of the system not because of the system.

Just consider some of the names in and around the England squad at the time:

- Martin Peters (Capt)
- Peter Shilton
- Roy McFarland
- Norman Hunter
- Colin Bell
- Paul Madeley
- Tony Currie
- Rodney Marsh
- Mick Channon
- Martin Chivers
- Allan Clarke
- Kevin Keegan
- Trevor Brooking.

Most of these players could have played in any international national team. This England team possessed more flair and natural ability than the 66 team. Colin Bell was at his best in 1973–74. He would drive teams forward almost on his own. When Czechoslovakia visited England at the start of the 1974–75 season – Revie's first match – Bell won the game almost on his own with his inspiration and two goals.

Roy McFarland was argued to be the most talented centre back

England had – some argued even more talented than the great Bobby Moore. Tony Currie had great creative flair and was a young emerging talent that excited crowds. Mick Channon was just emerging and was to become of stalwart of England in the mid-70s, scoring 21 goals in 46 games. He played during England's wilderness years. England's failure to qualify for three major international tournaments during Channon's career leaves him as the most-capped player never to have been named to a World Cup or European Championships squad. He remains joint 16th in the all-time England scorers list, level with Kevin Keegan.

The roll of honour goes on – Rodney Marsh too was entrancing fans throughout the country. Keegan too with his dynamic and forceful play. Martin Chivers was viewed to be a dangerous No 9 to match Geoff Hurst or Roger Hunt at their best, scoring 13 goals in 24 matches. Allan Clarke was an exceptional goalscorer. Shilton was to go on and become one of the greatest 'keeper's ever – not just English but throughout the world game.

Although England did go into decline after 73, there were glimpses of what could have been in the following year both under Joe Mercer when England played some exceptional football and even in the early days of Don Revie against Czechoslovakia and West Germany in 1975 when England won 2–0 with even more great names and players – Malcolm MacDonald, Colin Todd and Alan Hudson. At the time West Germany were the World Champions. The great Leeds team reached the European Cup of 1975. Liverpool won in 1977, 78 and 81. Nottingham Forest in 1979 and 1980. Aston Villa in 1982. England dominated the European Club stage for the next decade.

But the success on the club stage hid the truth. British club teams excelled for their attitude and spirit and this drove the club teams to success. On the international stage more was needed and time and again, the British teams flattered to deceive. In 1978, Scotland believed that they had a real chance to be successful at the World Cup in Argentina. When the moment came, they – just as England had many times – struggled and fell. Many turned on the Scottish manager, Ally McLeod, but the reality was the team was not prepared well enough for the challenge. The players were good enough but the system and structure of the game did not prepare the ground for International success.

This is not a story to cast blame, but to at long last, place some fair perspective and argue that England's players of 1974 were great players that could have had a golden era. It may be that regardless of this result, England were in decline, as we did not possess a winning mentality as an international team. England's club teams were about to start a Golden era between 1972–84 with Leeds (European Cup Finalists in 1975), Liverpool (European Cup winners in 77, 78, 81,84), the rise of Nottingham Forest (European Cup Winners in 1979 and 1980), Aston Villa (European Cup Winners in 1981), West Ham (European Cup Winners Cup Finalist in 1976), Tottenham Hotspur (1974 UEFA Cup Final, 1984 UEFA Cup winners), and Arsenal (European Cup Winners Cup Final in 1980).

The 1970s was a great era of football and not the bleak era of failure. This is a story of what could and should have been. It is story of human failure/error and one that affected a whole generation.

This story aims to set the record straight for Sir Alf and a great generation of players that could have been some of England's finest, but instead are footnotes to others. It is so often said that the game is about the players but there is far more to success than just having good players. Success on the international stage is also determined by mind-sets, fitness, preparation and tactics. The game was evolving across the world with the development of television. The English league matches were being watched all across the globe and inspiring footballers in many countries to learn and evolve – but had England's evolution stopped?

"What is forgotten is that football was not just about money in the old days; it was about communities. When Martin Peters led England out against Poland in 73, he was the captain of not 11 players but over 50 million people, all willing the team on. I find it so hard to listen to those that tell me that football is just a game. Of course, it is – but it was also the "escape" route" for millions from everyday life. It was far more import-ant that just a game.

Peter (Supporter).[4]

Focus group – London, March 2014.

1.

ENGLAND - ENGLAND'S RICH HERITAGE

When one supports England in football, one is committing to a relationship that swings to the extremes on the emotional scale. Balanced perspective is rare and hard to achieve. Even the most calm and considered men will be reduced to open displays of exasperation, anger and expressions of joy. If it were not such a testing journey, it would be almost funny and with moments of black humour. England, in its rich history, has boasted many great players but the national team has continuously flattered to deceive.

It is one of life's little ironies that the English are described as being an emotionally reserved race, for the truth is that the English are far more emotional than most nationalities. The English may be restrained with any open show of emotion in our day-to-day lives but that changes the moment they enter a sporting stadium. It is not just reserved for football; the English love their sport – all sports. It is no coincidence that after the Second World War, both football and cricket enjoyed periods when attendances reached new levels as people sought to escape their dismal daily hardships through sport. On August Bank Holiday Monday 1946, 100,000 attended nine first class cricket matches. In a friendly match between Chelsea and Dinamo Moscow in 1945 it is estimated that over 90,000 filled Stamford Bridge to watch a 3–3 draw. In theory, the gates were closed when an officially full capacity of 74,000 had entered but still thousands continued to enter the ground. The iconic Tommy Lawton was making his debut for Chelsea. It is estimated that nearly one million attended the opening matches of the season in 1946. Charlton, in

1946, attracted over 40,000 for each home match. At the time The Valley (Charlton's home stadium) was one of league's largest stadiums and for a match in 1938 versus Aston Villa had attracted a record 75,000 crowd. Football – and sport – had a new central importance within society.

The English have become increasingly competent in recent years – especially since lottery funding – at competing at the top levels across a wide range of sports; whether rugby, cricket, athletics, rowing, cycling, shooting, golf, tennis, sailing, hockey, lacrosse and more. The British love their sport and their fault is that they compete in so many. Most nations are committed to one or two – within Britain, there are many disciplines that take place on fields across the country every day. Sport does sit in the heart of every community.

The English are a nation with tribal passion at heart. Sport is where one can see the British really express themselves and be free in spirit. In football, one's team is one's tribe. It was Bill Shankly the great Liverpool manager of the 60s and early 70s who stated:

> "Some people believe football is a matter of life and death, I am very disappointed with that attitude. I can assure you it is much, much more important than that."[5]

Of course, it was tongue in cheek but Shankly understood more than most what football meant to the supporter standing on the terrace and he never took it lightly. England was a very different world in the 40s, 50s, 60s and 70s to what it is today. Football was about community and working class heroes. It was not the business that the large

---

5   *Daily Mail.* (2009) *Bill Shankly: The top 10 quotes of a Liverpool legend 50 years to the day since he took over.* [Online] Available from: http://www.dailymail.co.uk/sport/football/article-1232318/Bill-Shankly-The-quotes-Liverpool-legend-50-years-day-took-over.html [Accessed: 1 September 2014].

clubs are today. The connection between players and the supporters was deep and had importance. The Captain represented both the team and the community at large. He was their symbol. It is this very point that explains why the captain is seen to be such an important role even to this day. One will often read that the captain's role is often overstated. It is today, but it has a historic legacy when the captain's role was the more than just leading a football team. He was a working class hero from a community.

Bill Shankly was a man that could delight with his masterful use of humour as he would make the most telling point that would register with the listener –, just as when he commented:

> "A lot of football success is in the mind. You must believe you are the best and then make sure that you are. In my time at Liverpool we always said we had the best two teams on Merseyside, Liverpool and Liverpool Reserves".[6]

The English let their emotions go with sport. It touches the heart and soul. In sport, the English live every triumph and failure as though they were playing the game they are watching. Reserved Englishmen? Rudyard Kipling's famous words in the poem "IF" have a very special place in English culture. The words from the poem –

> "If you can meet with Triumph and Disaster and treat those two impostors just the same"[7]

6   *Daily Mail. (2009) Bill Shankly: The top 10 quotes of a Liverpool legend 50 years to the day since he took over.* [Online] Available from: http://www.dailymail.co.uk/sport/football/article-1232318/Bill-Shankly-The-quotes-Liverpool-legend-50-years-day-took-over.html [Accessed: 1st September 2014].

7   The Kipling Society – www.kiplingsociety.co.uk

are placed above the players entrance to centre court at Wimbledon. The words are used within schools to set the tone of what is English. However, with football, it seems they are often placed to one side.

IF

If you can keep your head when all about you
Are losing theirs and blaming it on you,
If you can trust yourself when all men doubt you,
But make allowance for their doubting too;
If you can wait and not be tired by waiting,
Or being lied about, don't deal in lies,
Or being hated, don't give way to hating,
And yet don't look too good, nor talk too wise:
If you can dream – and not make dreams your master;
If you can think – and not make thoughts your aim;
If you can meet with Triumph and Disaster
And treat those two impostors just the same;
If you can bear to hear the truth you've spoken
Twisted by knaves to make a trap for fools,
Or watch the things you gave your life to, broken,
And stoop and build 'em up with worn-out tools:

If you can make one heap of all your winnings
And risk it on one turn of pitch-and-toss,
And lose, and start again at your beginnings
And never breathe a word about your loss;
If you can force your heart and nerve and sinew
To serve your turn long after they are gone,
And so hold on when there is nothing in you
Except the Will which says to them: 'Hold on!'

If you can talk with crowds and keep your virtue,

Or walk with Kings – nor lose the common touch,

if neither foes nor loving friends can hurt you,

If all men count with you, but none too much;

If you can fill the unforgiving minute

With sixty seconds' worth of distance run,

Yours is the Earth and everything that's in it,

And – which is more – you'll be a Man, my son![8]

We stay true to only very few of these words and maybe football is our escapism and we place the need to be men to one side and let our childish nature loose when we enter the arena. We rarely keep our heads when others are losing theirs; we are desperately impatient, and we can hate with a frightening intensity.

Yes, we can certainly dream and we can walk with Kings and the common man – as long as they share our dream and team. But dreams do master us and we certainly are unable to handle triumph and disaster as just being imposters. Our foes do hurt us and as for forgiveness ... that is extremely hard.

The gentleman and football are not bedfellows. This is not through a lack of good intent – just that our tribe's champions are in battle and we support them with our heart and soul. The football fan is a passionate being and, with England, that passion is tested.

England's history is dominated by great triumphs that make us believe we can be Champions of the World and moments of shock when our dreams and illusions are shattered. One thing is certainly true – it is never dull when supporting England. We have had victories against the odds. We have had players that make you jump to your feet and shout out loud. We have moments of disbelief and embarrassment that can bring tears.

---

8   http://www.kiplingsociety.co.uk/poems_if.htm (online).

It is often said that England is arrogant in its belief that we are better than we are and that is based on the fact that England invented the game. Regardless of the merits of this argument, England's history does deserve respect. It is an easy argument to say that England is arrogant. As with most things, the truth is more complex and grey than simple black and white extremes.

There is an argument that England could really have been genuine world champions for long periods between 1870 and 1950. Without consistent international tournaments it is impossible to answer this question, but England won the football gold medal in the 1908 and 1912 Olympics and it seems clear no other nation had overtaken England by this point. How they would have coped with the 1920s Uruguayans or travelling to and playing in South America in 1930 raises some doubts, but it could be argued that they were the best team in Europe, if not the world, in the 1940s and before this may have even have won one or both of the 1934 or 1938 World Cups had they competed. Is it too much to suggest that if there had been a European-based World Cup in the 1940s then England would surely have won it?

This claim to greatness is chiefly substantiated by England's results against Italy, still reigning World Champions until 1950, and still under the guidance of the great coach, Pozzo, in 1948. Italy never beat England when they were World Champions and on 16 May 1948 England beat the Italians 4–0 in Turin. The Italy team contained seven players from the great Torino side of the era. This was seen as a major victory at the time and justified England's high opinion of her own footballers. Also in 1948 England beat Portugal an incredible 10–0 away in Lisbon. This was a Portuguese side that had recently ended the record unbeaten run of the great emerging Hungarian side. And, of course, England remained unbeaten at Wembley until

1953 when the Hungarian team of Puskas came to Wembley and won over the nation with their natural flair and skill. The Hungarians, on that day in 1953, showed England that the game was changing and evolving with new ideas, tactics and approach.

It is important to place into perspective why the woes of the 1970s were important by touching on England's great history and by illustrating some of the great matches and players over the years. The following are brief synopsis of the matches that will always be recognised in history and include the day when England played the World Champions, Italy, in 1934; the day England beat the Germans in 1938, just prior to the Second World War; the day that shook England as they lost to the United States in the Brazil World Cup of 1950; the 1953 match v Hungary and of course the Final of 66 and the famous match versus Brazil in 1970. These matches will always stand the test of time and stand highlighted in England's history whatever happens from this day forth.

THE HISTORICAL MATCHES

November 1934 • The Battle of Highbury • England v Italy
England played the newly crowned World Champions at Arsenal's stadium in north London in a tense and often bad tempered match. England had not taken part in the 1934 World Cup so the match has special meaning. England to measure how they fared against the best team in the world and for the Italians to prove conclusively that deserved the title World Champions. England went 3–0 in the first 12 minutes through goals from Eric Brook (3 and 10 mins) and Ted Drake (12). The Italians though were not World Champions for nothing and came back in the second half with goals through Guiseppe Meazza (58 and 62). Stanley Matthews later recounted it was one of

the most violent matches he had ever played in and Italy did play most of the game with only 10 fit men after their centre-half, Monti, had his foot broken after only two minutes.

Sir Winston Churchill once said, "Italians lose wars as if they were football matches, and football matches as if they were wars."[9]

September 1938 • Germany v England

With war looming, England played Germany in Berlin in front of a crowd of 110,000. Despite the players' reluctance, the Foreign office ordered the players to show respect to their hosts with the Nazi salute prior to the match. Stanley Matthews later recalled:

> "The dressing room erupted. There was bedlam. All the England players were livid and totally opposed to this, myself included. Everyone was shouting at once. Eddie Hapgood, normally a respectful and devoted captain, wagged his finger at the official and told him what he could do with the Nazi salute, which involved putting it where the sun doesn't shine."[10]

None the less, it clearly motivated the players to show less respect during the match as an England team inspired by the great Stanley Matthews outplayed Germany to win 6–3 through goals from Cliff Bastin, Jackie Robinson, Stanley Matthews, Frank Broome and Len Goulden.

The game was watched by 110,000 people as well as senior Nazis,

---

9   *The Guardian*. (2008) *Is English football really the best in Europe?* [Online] Available from: http://www.theguardian.com/football/2008/apr/01/europeanfootball.sport1 [Accessed: 21 November 2014].

10   This Day in Football History. (2010) *14 May 1938 – Hapgood Had The Right Idea*. [Online] Available from: http://tdifh.blogspot.co.uk/2010/05/14-may-1938-hapgood-had-right-idea.html [Accessed: 10 November 2014].

Hermann Göring and Joseph Goebbels. England won the game 6–3. The game included a goal scored by Len Goulden that Stanley Matthews described as, "the greatest goal I ever saw in football". According to Matthews:

"Len met the ball on the run; without surrendering any pace, his left leg cocked back like the trigger of a gun, snapped forward and he met the ball full face on the volley. To use modern parlance, his shot was like an Exocet missile. The German goalkeeper may well have seen it coming, but he could do absolutely nothing about it. From 25 yards the ball screamed into the roof of the net with such power that the netting was ripped from two of the pegs by which it was tied to the crossbar."[11]

29 June 1950 • The Day that Shook England to the core • The 1950 World Cup group Stages • USA v England
England first played in the 1950 World Cup and in a match they were expected to easily win they fielded a side that included Bert Williams, Alf Ramsey, the Captain Billy Wright, Jimmy Dickenson, Stan Mortensen and Tom Finney; some great names and players but yet England managed to lose 1–0 through a goal from Joseph Gaetjens on 38 minutes. When England had beaten Italy 4–0 in 1948, it was felt we were World Champion contenders and two years later we had lost to an amateur footballing nation. Our inner confidence was suddenly punctured and the 1950s were a period of some difficulty. Bert Williams, the England and Wolverhampton goalkeeper was later to say:

---

11   Spartacus Educational. (2014) *West Ham United Biographies: Len Goulden.* [Online] Available from: http://spartacus-educational.com/ WHgouldenL.htm [Accessed: 21 November 2014].

"But you've got to give the Americans some credit for what they did. As soon as an English player picked up the ball, everyone in the American side retreated into their goalmouth. You couldn't see the goals for legs."[12]

25 November 1953 • The Day Modern Football began
• England v Hungary

In front of 100,000 people at the old Wembley Stadium an England team was outplayed by a Hungary team that played a new, more modern brand of football than had been seen before. It was a match that confirmed England's decline as a world power but also excited many observers with the skill and approach of a very skilful Hungarian team led by the great Ferenc Puskas. The story grew worse as England lost the return match in May 1954 7–1 in front of 92,000 in Nepstadion.

30 July 1966 • World Champions • England v Germany

Every England supporter knows the story of Geoff Hurst's hat-trick and how England won the World Cup at Wembley Stadium. Led by the young, charismatic Bobby Moore and with a team that included the great Gordon Banks, Martin Peters, Alan Ball, and Bobby Charlton, England at last fulfilled the dreams of English fans as they resisted the stubborn resistance of a very capable West German team. Germany scored first through Helmut Haller but by half-time, England had wrestled control through goals from Hurst and Peters. Webber then equalised in the last seconds of the match, which led to the dramatic twists of Hurst's third goal, which bounced off the underside of the bar onto the line. Was it a goal or not? The debate

---

12   BBC Sport. (2010) *Defeat by US still hurts, says England old boy Williams.* [Online] Available from: http://news.bbc.co.uk/sport1/hi/football/ world_cup_2010/8728535.stm [Accessed: 22 October 2014].

has raged on for years but Hurst's third goal was worthy of winning a match. Bobby Moore's calmness under pressure, his long pass to Hurst. Hurst's run toward goal and how he hit his shot beyond the German 'keeper with raw power.

England may have had better players but the England team of 66 will always be the benchmark as it combined truly world-class players with good players such as Jack Charlton, Nobby Stiles, George Cohen, Roger Hunt and Ray Wilson to create a real team that faced moments of adversity, pressure, great play, aggression and still came through.

7 June 1970 • A Game for the Memory • England v Brazil

In the group stages of the 1970 World Cup in Mexico, England faced the favourites Brazil in the second match. It is a game that is generally regarded as one of the greatest of England's games as it included some inspiring moments such as Banks "wonder" save from a Pele header and Moore's calm tackle of Jairzinho in full flight. Brazil went on to win the World Cup playing some of the most exciting and free flowing football ever seen. No team came close to beating them bar England who should have drawn the match save for Jeff Astle missing an open goal. But that is sport.

The game though is remembered for two great moments. The first when Brazil broke to the by-line and crossed for the rising Pele to head the ball with all his power towards the goal from 10 yards from the goal. The great player cried "Goal" as the ball left his head. Probably every supporter in the stadium, in Brazil and in England thought it was to be a goal but Banks, who had been on the near post, flew his body through the air to tip the ball over the bar. Bobby Charlton described it as, "the greatest save I have seen". It was one of those sporting moments that makes you stop in your tracks and respect the moment whichever side you may support.

In the second moment, the great Jairzinho – one of the players of the 1970 tournament – picked the ball up and ran with guile and speed at the England Penalty area. Only Moore stood in his way. Bobby waited with calm authority as the Brazilian attacked. Moore waited and then slid his foot in and stopped Jairzinho in his tracks. It was like a young boxer attacking an older, fading champion but the experience and skill of the latter won the moment.

It has often been argued that the England team of 1970 was a better team than the 1966 team. Did this hold validity? Charlton was still a powerful player, even though in his last days. Banks and Moore had reached their peaks as had Peters and Ball. They had been joined by Alan Mullery, Terry Cooper, Brian Labone, Keith Newton and Francis Lee who were seen as more skilful players than the ones they had replaced. This was one of England's greatest teams.

14 June 1970 • West Germany v England
• The World Cup Quarter Final

England were confident after the group stages and it was generally felt that England and Brazil would meet again in the Final. In the first hour of the match there was little to dispel this belief as Mullery (32) and Peter (50) scored. England looked destined for the semi-finals and Sir Alf Ramsey clearly believed so as he withdrew Bobby Charlton from the game to save him for the semis but this let Germany back in with goals from Beckenbauer (69) and Seeler (82) to take the game to extra-time.

England now were in trouble. The great Gordon Banks has been taken ill in the morning and replaced by his Chelsea understudy – Peter Bonetti – a goalkeeper known as "The cat" in England but in this game he was at error for the second goal and England's confidence seemed to wilt. They had also replaced two of their true world-class players in Charlton and Martin Peters. Most experts focus on Charlton's withdraw was being the cause of England's fall in the match but Peter's substitution was just as important, as Peters carried threat and was such an athletic player. Norman Hunter replaced him and England were now a defensive outfit. Momentum had changed and it was only a matter of time before the great Gerd Muller scored (108). Again Bonetti was arguably at fault, but England's fate had been sealed.

The Champions

The 1970 exit from the World Cup should have marked the end of an era and the breakup of the team with an eye on the World Cup in Germany, but Ramsey was a loyal man and was to remain steadfastly by those that had won him the World Cup. It is easy to say that this was a mistake, but maybe he knew that in Moore, Ball, Hurst and Peters he still possessed four men who along with Banks were world-class. Maybe he recognised that England had a mental fragility on the world stage and he wanted experience and a winning psychology around him as he prepared to evolve the side?

It is also easy to be critical with hindsight. Hindsight is a great gift for all historians but England; in all sports seem to struggle with being World Champions. There does appear to be a weakness in the England psyche, which suggests that the mind-set is one of achieving the goal rather than possessing the ruthless streak that allows the team to thrive as the number one side in the world. It is just a consistent theme that spreads across English sport. The England Rugby Union World Cup winning team soon lost its way after 2003 and declined in authority within months. The same can be said of the England Cricket team that reached number one in the world in 2011. It was no different for England's football team after 1966.

One would have hoped that the 1966 triumph marked a time for celebration and that the team would kick on to great things. Without question, the team had presence and would bully lesser teams, but would be fragile against those teams that dared to challenge their position and authority. Was it really any coincidence that the first team to beat the World Champions was Scotland at Wembley in a deserved 3–2 victory. Scotland would not have wilted in the presence of England. In fact, their team probably grew in confidence wanting to be the first to dance the victory jig over the World Champions.

England fielded all their winning team bar Roger Hunt who had been replaced by a goal scoring legend in Jimmy Greaves. Scotland's finest on that April day in 1967 included some combative players who would never take a backward step – Billy Bremner, Dennis Law, John Greig, Eddie McCreadie, Jim Baxter, Jim McCalliog and Bobby Lennox. England will point to an injury to Jackie Charlton that caused England to be weakened that day, as Jack Charlton ended up having to play in attack but such injuries happen and the question is how every team copes when things go wrong. England began pointing to excuses rather than just dealing with what was happening and playing what was unfolding in front of them.

In fairness, Scottish football was at its height, with Celtic in May 1967 becoming the first British side to win the European Cup. Scotland were a good team that had under achieved at international level. The result against England gave the nation a lift and one could even pose the question as to whether Scotland's finest beating England in April gave Celtic the confidence to win is Lisbon a month later?

However, England should still have not lost. They were the Champions and Scotland had not even qualified. The match was not even a friendly but a full competitive match in a European Championships qualification group. However, England did – with luck – manage to regroup and progress through the group, beat Spain – home and away – in the quarter-finals and faced Yugoslavia in the semi-finals in Florence (Italy).

Just as England had struggled in 67 with Scotland's aggression, so Yugoslavia brought a physical and aggressive game to Florence. The game is best remembered for Alan Mullery being the first England player to be red carded, but the truth is that England had fallen into the trap of playing the physical game that Yugoslavia had wanted and lost by the single goal. Faced with a similar approach in 66 (against Argentina), England had found a way through. Now they had lost a game they should have won. Alan Mullery was later to describe the event that had him sent off:

"Every Yugoslavian player that day spent the whole game kicking all of us, but this one guy – Dobrivoje Trivic – he was the worst. He was quite exceptional. We were losing 1–0 with about a minute to go and this coward – and that's what he was, because he wouldn't confront people, he'd just kick them from behind – had a go at me. He raked his studs, whatever they were made of, down my calf. Blood started pouring out, and I just turned around and kicked him in the how's your fathers.

The referee was about two yards away. If I'd realised he was that close I probably wouldn't have done it, but it was sheer frustration. Of course he shows me the red card and I'm off. I had no idea at the time that no England player had ever been sent off; it never even entered my head. It was a moment of anger and frustration, but I've had to live with it for so many years now.

Nobby Stiles was on the bench, and he walked with me

off the pitch. Just as we were going down the tunnel we heard the whistle blow. We got to the dressing room just before the rest of the team, and I got in the bath as quickly as possible. The next thing, Alf was coming into the dressing room and he wasn't very happy to be fair. But he wasn't particularly unhappy with me, he was unhappy with the way the Yugo-slavians had kicked lumps out of us all game, and the referee who never did anything about it.

He had a few harsh words with me for what I'd done, but I've got to say he was very, very good with me. He stood up for me after that – he even paid the fifty pounds I was fined by the FA. He was very strong for his players, was Alf, and that's why any player that ever played for Alf Ramsey, they all loved him. He was a player's manager."[13]

It was England's fragility in the big matches that was their Achilles heel and Ramsey knew it. He knew he had to find a solution and he thought the best way was by retaining those that had been proven winners around the team?

There was an interesting conundrum that was developing – the English league was renowned for its tough, physical approach and yet England were struggling against teams that were overly aggressive in their approach. England would play their best football against those that played passing football. England could be intimidated, which is strange given the intensity of league matches each week. This "weak-ness" would come back to haunt them in the match in June 1973 in Poland, a game where the Poles took the rules to the limit. One would have thought, of all teams that the English would be able to

13   *The Guardian.* (2010) *5 June 1968: Ramsey pays for England's first ever red card.* [Online] Available from: http://www.theguardian.com/sport/2009/jun/06/england-first-red-card-mullery [Accessed: 21 November 2014].

handle hostile aggressive teams, but maybe the problem lay in the fact that the English generally played tough but fair and struggled when it went a step beyond? This is hard to accept given some of the aggression that one could see during Football League matches. Maybe England felt that they were one of the world's best teams and should play above the rough and ready? That they believed that their "class" would tell in the end?

Ramsey had played during the difficult years of the 1950s and had understood that international tournaments were not always won by great players, but with great teams who were mentally strong. Few would ever doubt the passion and determination of any England team nor the potential that lay within the players, but for some reason, England's teams lacked the mental strength and calmness in the big matches to overcome moments, which invariably would go against them, when playing the best teams. They would not mentally fold like some teams would. They would strive and work with all their might but they lacked a calmness and inner belief to steer themselves through a crisis.

The team of 66 was different in that they had the players who were both technically brilliant but also those that would relish a contest and would not be intimidated. The team mixed the beauty with the beast and they had a team for all occasions. England had a World Class goalkeeper with the class of Bobby Moore leading a mobile defensive unit. Jack Charlton played to ensure Moore was covered if he made a rare mistake, as Ramsey knew Charlton would take no prisoners. Jack Charlton may have lacked natural skill at the highest level but he would never be intimidated, nor take a backward step. He was an ideal foil for the technical class of Moore. In front of the back four, stood England's most under rated player – Nobby Stiles – who feared no one and was ready for whatever came his way.

In midfield, he mixed the youth of Ball and Peters with the experience of Bobby Charlton and Stiles. Charlton could turn a game on its head with his running and shooting. He would excite crowds and strike fear into the opposition who would have to have a defensive plan just for Charlton's storming runs. Few midfield players have ever carried the same threat as Charlton did at his peak. One could argue that Charlton's loss from the international stage changed the dynamic of playing England, as teams could be more aggressive in their approach. Charlton was one of England's greatest ever players. It was unlikely he could be replaced with ease, although Bell, at his best, was a good replacement who was improving as an international player Currie in 73 possessed the potential to light up the international stage.

Upfront Ramsey played two strikers with a great team work ethic. Hurst and Hunt were team players and good goalscorers. Many will say that Greaves was the more talented player but Greaves was a fan's player who did not possess the inner strength that Hurst possessed. Greaves was the more gifted player and his overall record as a striker is better than Hurst's but Hurst was a team player with an excellent temperament and spirit.

In 1966, one of the great debates in the tournament had been over Jimmy Greaves not beings selected for the Final as Ramsey kept faith with Hurst. Greaves was one of England's finest and a proven goalscorer but it was often felt that Ramsey had question marks over Greaves. It is hard to know if this was true for Hurst had performed well in Greaves absence and it would have been a risk to select Greaves for the Final when he had not played for two weeks. Ramsey was pragmatic. Some say he did not trust flair players but he did. He just understood what created a winning team and that this lay in the psychology of the side.

Arguably England, over their history, have lacked that inner confidence at international level to make them move from being quarter-finalists to contenders. England had fallen in 1950, 1954 (QF v Uruguay), 1958 (even though England had just lost great players in the Munich air crash including Duncan Edwards) and in 1962 (QF v Brazil). A pattern was clear. Ramsey had found a solution and even though the problem still was evident, was it not understandable that he was loath to jettison his winners as he built a new side?

"It is a football match, not a war. Let us keep our sense of perspective – everybody is getting hysterical. If we do lose, the game is not going to die. It will be a terrible thing for six weeks and then everybody will forget about it."[14]

Alan Hardaker (FA Secretary in a Radio Interview 1973).

14   *The Guardian*. (2005) *Semi-final or bust for Sven, pay-off permitting.* [Online] Available from: http://www.theguardian.com/football/2005/oct/08/ sport.comment3 [Accessed: 28 August 2014].

2.

THE ROAD TO 1973

If fate had not dealt its cruel hand with the great loss of life in the Munich air crash of 58, it is very feasible that England would have had a competitive team in the 1962 World Cup with Duncan Edwards and some of the "Busby Babes" such as Tommy Taylor, Mark Jones and David Pegg. These were seen to be some of England's finest young talent to come through and it appeared that success was their destiny. 1958 would still have been early in their development but by 1962, these players could have joined the likes of Johnny Haynes, Jimmy Greaves, Bobby Moore, Ray Wilson, Bobby Charlton, Jimmy Armfield and Bobby Robson to form a formidable England team. The whole of the 1960s could have been a golden age for the England side, led by Duncan Edwards. Edwards was an awe-inspiring player who possessed both strength and skill. He had become the heartbeat and leader of the Busby babes that were winning admirers across Europe. The 1962 World Cup in Chile would have been his stage.

But fate did change destiny's course and England were a solid side in 62 but not more. Every great side needs five world-class players and three great talents. The 1966 had five world-class players in Bobby Moore, Gordon Banks, Bobby Charlton, Martin Peters and Ray Wilson. The three great talents were Alan Ball, Geoff Hurst and Ray Wilson. In 62, England could have had five world-class players in Haynes, Charlton, Moore, Edwards, and Greaves. These five would match in talent the five from 66. Then add in the possible strengths of Mark Jones, David Pegg, Tommy Taylor, and Bobby Robson and it could have been a very special team.

The road to the 1966 triumph had begun back in the mid 50s with the rise of a new generation of class players led by the likes of Duncan Edwards, and Johnny Haynes. The Hungarian win in 1953 at Wembley may have shocked many but is also inspired a new generation to develop and hone their skills. The Hungarians showed a new dimension to the game and, although there was no joy in losing to the Hungarians, the English did take note and learn lessons. The Busby babes excited many across England as they developed and would have provided England with a strong talent base, able to compete in 62, bar the Munich air crash but the seeds had been sown and success was achieved in 66.

The early 70s too boasted many great players that had taken on the mantle – Francis Lee, Alan Mullery, Terry Cooper, Colin Bell, Peter Osgood, Allan Clarke, Alan Hudson, Norman Hunter, Martin Chivers, and Peter Shilton. Many argue that the 1970 World Cup team could – and should – have contested the Final against Brazil. They should certainly have closed out the game against West Germany but Italy would have offered a stern test in the semi-finals. The England team had its five world-class players and more in Banks, Moore, Peters, Bobby Charlton, Alan Ball and Geoff Hurst and its three great talents in Terry Cooper – who many regarded as the best left back in the Mexico finals – Alan Mullery and Francis Lee.

They were a strong, combative unit but truth is that had spluttered and flattered to deceive in 1970. Results from that year indicated the reality that came to pass. England did not play well and arguably were a team in decline. If one looks at their results against teams that did not even qualify for the World Cup in 1970, it did indicate that England would struggle against the best teams as came to pass.

14 January 1970 – England 0 Netherlands 0

25 February 1970 – Belgium 1 England 3

18 April 1970 – Wales 1 England 1

21 April 1970 – England 3 Northern Ireland 1

25 April 1970 – Scotland 0 England 0[15]

Three draws out of five games did suggest that England had vulnerability or at least a struggle to turn draws into wins. Although England won two of their three group games in the World Cup, it was only by the odd goal. Teams that compete for the World Cup generally put lesser opponents to the sword but this was not happening.

There is no question England raised their game and excelled against Brazil in one of the great games for the 1970 World Cup. Although it was a great disappointment that England went out in the style they did, all the warning lights had been flashing for some time and maybe it was time to rebuild. Ramsey was a pragmatist and would have known England's vulnerability. He began the process of evolving the team almost straight away as he brought in new players to test their ability but with the safeguard of the proven still around to provide leadership.

However, one has to note that it was a different era and the England manager had far less room for error against the England manager of today. In the early 70s, the England team played less games and England had only one friendly International before they started their European Nations Cup campaign. This was against East Germany and Ramsey played 4–3–3 with the trusted strike force of Lee and Hurst upfront with Allan Clarke. Peter Shilton played his first senior International and David Sadler and Emlyn Hughes were brought into a revamped backline. England won easily enough 3–1 with goals from Lee, Peters and Clarke.

---

15   http://www.englandfc.com/nostal/nostalgia.html

In their first competitive match, Ramsey experimented further by giving a new strike force a chance in Joe Royle (Everton) and Martin Chivers (Spurs). Admittedly the game was against Malta so not the most testing of opponents but it showed that Ramsey was intent on building a new team. Also in that match, he played Paul Reaney (Leeds), Roy McFarland (Derby) and Colin Harvey (Everton). However the difficult of Ramsey's role was shown by a solitary 1–0 win with a goal from the trusted Peters.

The next game was against Greece at Wembley and Ramsey returned to his trusted players to ensure victory by playing Banks, Moore, Ball, Peters, Hurst, and Lee. Yes Chivers played again and scored the opening goal in a 3–0 win. Yes he played other new players in the likes of Peter Storey, the tough no nonsense Arsenal hard man, but Ramsey knew his trusted players would find victory. In the next match against Malta at Wembley, the team sheet again boasted Banks, Moore, Ball, Peters, Lee as the backbone. Chivers played again alongside Clarke and Lee. Ralph Coates (the spurs winger/midfielder) was given his opportunity along with the Liverpool full-back, Chris Lawler. England won at a canter, – 5-0 – being 4–0 up by the 48th minute through Chivers (2), Lee and Clarke. Lawler scored in the 75th minute. It was gradual steady evolution but with the trusted backbone from 66.

England completed the first season after the World Cup with a 1–0 win against Northern Ireland, a 0–0 draw with Wales at Wembley and then a 3–1 win against the Scots at Wembley. The Wales match saw Ramsey being unusually radical by playing the Liverpool back four in Lawler, Hughes, Tommy Smith and Larry Lloyd but Ramsey liked solid units. Against Scotland, he returned to his trusted of Banks, Moore, Ball, Peters, Lee and Hurst. Chivers scored twice – along with a goal from Peters – to firmly establish his place in

Ramsey's new era. Chris Lawler played too and seemed to be part of the new side, as did Roy McFarland.

The personnel may not have changed much but the system had – Ramsey had won the World Cup with 4–4–2 but was now playing a more ambitious 4–3–3 – three strikers and one less player in midfield. In fairness to Ramsey, his teams were bold and aggressive as Peters was a natural goalscorer too and Bell – when he played – and Ball were attacking minded players. It maybe that Ramsey changed his system as he could see that England had struggled to outplay and put lesser teams away but the counter is that it did place more pressure of the defensive line and this was not as settled as in his great teams.

As the next season started, the old trusted guard continued with Banks, Moore, Hurst, Ball, Lee and Peters against Switzerland, and Greece. But then in April 1972 the dangers of this policy became all too obvious as England were outplayed at Wembley by their old foes, West Germany in the quarter-finals of the European Championships. This match really marked the beginning of the end for Ramsey, although of course, this was not known at the time.

29 April 1972. • England v West Germany
England: Banks, Moore, Hunter, Hughes, Madeley, Ball, Peters, Bell, Hurst, Lee and Chivers.

It was an attack-focused team but the weaknesses of his trusted old guard were evident as the team were outplayed during the match. Many remember the game for the West German midfielder Gunter Netzer dominating the midfield but the 4–3–3 strategy allowed Netzer the space and he accepted the gift with pleasure. McIlvanney wrote in his match report for *The Observer*, "No Englishman can ever again warm himself with the old assumption that, on the football field if nowhere else, the Germans are an inferior race".[16]

The simple truth was that the Germans had grown since the World Cup and England had slipped back as their world-class players had become the old guard. Germany were building their own World Cup wining team and arguably the team was stronger in 1972 than it was in 1974. They were at their peak. England, though, were a declining force that lacked the presence that they possessed less than two years earlier.

It has to said that England placed themselves under pressure during the game. The first goal – from Hoeness on 26 minutes – came from Bobby Moore trying to dribble his way out of trouble in the England box and making an extremely poor pass. Great sportsmen often struggle to realise their powers are on the wane in their latter years. They seem to believe that they can still play as they did at their height and it is common that such players make poor errors as they try to prove themselves. It is as though they try to impose themselves by doing that bit extra. This was one prime example, as the Moore of 1970 would have cleared the ball after he beat the first player, rather than make an elementary mistake, which led directly to the goal. Hurst too was ineffectual up front and the Germans seemed to have the game under control.

England equalised in the 77th minute but again, shot themselves in the foot with a needless penalty in the 84th. It can be argued that the tackle was outside the area but the truth is that it was Moore who was beaten for speed.

Hugh McIlvaney wrote:

---

16   McIlvanney, H. (1973) England shown the way out. *The Guardian.* [Online] 2011. Available from: http://observer.theguardian.com/englandfootball/ story/0,9565,541541,00.html. [Accessed: 11 October 2014].

"Last night at Wembley a West German team playing with grace and spirit and an absolute commitment to attack administered the most thorough defeat ever inflicted on Sir Alf Ramsey's England on their own ground. This, the first victory any German side has won over England in this country, was undeniably deserved.

It makes the personal score between Ramsey and Helmut Schoen, West Germany's coach, 3–3 but Schoen has now had three successes in a row and he is clearly in the ascendant. He will go into the second leg of this European Nations' Cup quarter-final in Berlin two weeks from now confident of winning on aggregate.

The German decision to choose a team geared to aggression was vindicated long before the interval. Once they had emerged from the panicky turmoil induced in their defence by England's opening assault, they settled to play composed, intelligent but surging ambitious football.

Almost immediately they strengthened the misgivings about the wisdom of Sir Alf Ramsey's unexpected policy of manning the midfield with three players noted for what they can do with the ball, rather than what they can do to get it. If that policy had been a failure in Athens earlier in the competition, now it was a disaster.

The boldness involved in omitting a hard physical competitor such as Mullery or Storey might have been less severely punished if Bell had been at his most thrusting and dominating. But the Manchester City man was a displaced person much of the time. And all his straining efforts to impose an influence could not reduce his remoteness from the vital areas of action.

Ball, flourishing his fist at members of his own team who appeared less than utterly resolute and occasionally flourishing studs at Germans who came in his way, did his best to promote an English takeover in the middle of the field. But neither he nor Peters could subdue the creative alliance of Netzer, Hoeness and Wimmer.

These three are not merely exceptional players. They are marvellously complementary. Throughout the first half Wimmer used his strength and pace to carry the ball with menacing swiftness out of defence, and the inspired Netzer was always available to explode out of his normal strolling gait into a thrilling penetrating gallop.

Hoeness adds an incisive positional sense to his fine technique and unselfish mobility and he made difficulties for England wherever he appeared. He was particularly damaging when moving wide to support the runs of Grabowski and Held.

Against such well-conceived attacking, England's full-backs could be forgiven their not infrequent moments of uneasiness.

Both Madeley and Hughes (though he fully earned Ramsey's praise) had ample reason to be grateful that Hunter was covering with a consuming vigour. The Leeds defender devoted much of his energy to policing Muller, but he had an adequate overspill to discourage any other German forward who came within reach of that steel claw of a left leg.

Nevertheless Moore, with his natural tendency to stand off forwards, missed the help of an intimidating contact player, such as Jack Charlton, at centre-half.

Yet it was hard to anticipate just how serious his problems

would be when his team began confidently on a Wembley pitch left as lush as an Irish meadow by the rain that returned during the match.

It seemed a happy omen when Beckenbauer, the German captain, was the first to be disconcerted by England's initial pressure. Beckenbauer was flustered into misdirecting a bad pass to Lee and there followed almost a minute of hectic confusion in which Chivers, Bell and Lee himself went frustratingly close to scoring. Maier gained respite at last by dropping on a shot from Bell and both Beckenbauer and his goalkeeper were brilliant from then on.

Any Englishman who felt there was to be slaughtering revenge for that afternoon in Leon two years ago was soon disillusioned as the Germans began to attack with sweeping elegance.

One graceful German move gave Grabowski an opening for a fierce shot from 25 yards. A deflection off Hunter might have meant trouble, but instead it lifted the ball over the crossbar. From the corner Banks punched the ball perilously close to Muller's feet without paying a penalty.

England were not, of course, subdued. Hughes, taking a return pass on the edge of the area, was obliged to shoot with his left foot. It is his weaker one, but the shot was powerful enough to look deadly when the ball ricocheted off Beckenbauer's back. Maier was in contorted disarray until it landed on the top of his net.

Netzer again alarmed England with a magnificently direct run that took him all of 50 yards and into the heart of the opposition's territory before he slid the ball short to Muller. Muller succeeded in squeezing a shot through

Hughes's legs, but Banks scrambled the ball wide for a corner.

The goalkeeper's relief was sadly temporary. In the twenty-seventh minute Moore loitered over a clearance and permitted Muller and Held, to make room for Hoeness in an inside-left position. Hoeness struck a sudden right foot shot from 20 yards, and the ball spun off Hunter and flew viciously past Banks's right side and into the net.

Lee, who had started unimpressively, was now more assertive and after misusing a chance for a scoring header by the far post he met a headed clearance with a great falling volley. Maier's save, like all his work, was admirable.

Peters, first from 25 yards and then from almost on the goalline, nearly scored towards the end of the half, but the Germans were soon flooding towards Banks again.

England restarted forcefully, but their front men were no more convincing than those in midfield. Chivers had a shot charged down and from Hughes's cross Hurst drove high over, left footed. But the German's were quickly rolling the ball around with their first half assurance and skill.

When Madeley slipped to let Muller into the left-hand corner of the penalty area, Hunter surged across to scramble the ball away. Muller dived, more in hope than anything else, but the referee was in no mood to be generous.

Hughes, put though by Ball, got in a dangerous cross, which was turned for a corner by Breitner, and as England began to batter away at the mass of green shirts, the crowd repeated their earlier demands for Rodney Marsh. This time they got him, Hurst being withdrawn for the Manchester City forward. At once England were galvanised. Madeley slipped

Grabowski and fed Bell, but his pass left Ball with too sharp an angle to evade Maier's arms.

With Hughes and Madeley now fully committed to attacking support, Germany were pinned back for the first time since the opening minutes.

England nearly took the goal they were chasing when, from Moore's cross. Hughes met the ball briskly, left-footed on the half volley, but it struck the top of the crossbar and bounced over.

Another deep, searching cross from Moore was met by Peter's head and Maier had to plunge anxiously to his right to hold the ball. With the free-kicks coming more rapidly, Madeley brought down Muller with a tackle, which had the German press box seats thumping in anger.

One piece of jugglery by Marsh failed to bring a profitable response from Bell; and when Maier finally lost a high centre, Marsh himself saw his looping header easily cleared from near the line by Hottges.

Though it seemed unlikely that England's aggression would produce a goal, they equalised dramatically in the seventy-sixth minute. Ball fouled Wimmer, badly, but the referee astonishingly waved play on. The Arsenal man moved the ball forward to Bell, who exchanged passes with Peters before striking a fierce angled shot which Maier could only beat down. This time the ball bounced towards the far post, where Lee joyfully ran it and himself into the back of the net.

England were level for only seven minutes. Their understandable willingness to thrust players forward always made them vulnerable to the German capacity for sudden breaks.

Held was often prominent in these and now he went sprinting wide of Moore on the left wing.

As Held veered towards Banks, Moore with his last stretching attempt at a tackle brought the forward down heavily. English complaints about the award of a penalty were no more sustained than they had right to be.

Banks's unique ability merely made the penalty a more miserable experience for England. Lunging instantly to the right as Netzer made contact with the ball, the goalkeeper pushed it on to the post, but it spun back behind his right shoulder and England seemed halfway out of the Nations Cup.

The worst defeat a Ramsey team have ever suffered at Wembley was given its final shape two minutes from the finish. A thrown pass from Banks in response to Hughes's call was badly fumbled by the back and Held readily dispossessed him. The ball was moved on to Hoeness and he ran across the edge of the area, staying just clear of Hunter's challenge."[17]

The return match was two weeks later and it has always been said that Ramsey picked a very defensive team fearing heavy defeat. It was certainly a tougher defensive team with two of England's toughest players in Norman Hunter and Peter Storey both of whom had reputations for taking no prisoners. But Ramsey's selection also showed a deep uncertainty in his thinking as he played the no nonsense approach of these two coupled with the grace and skill of Moore and McFarland and then in Rodney Marsh he played one of England's new breed of skilled mavericks who were exciting crowds all round the country but why play such a player in a team with such little creativity?

---

17   McIlvanney, H. (1973) England shown the way out. *The Guardian.* [Online] 2011. Available from: http://observer.theguardian.com/englandfootball/story/0,9565,541541,00.html [Accessed: 11 October 2014].

It was clear that Ramsey had called time on Geoff Hurst but he still retained faith in his captain Moore. Peters who was still playing excellent football sat on the bench. Peters could have a great foil and support for the inexperienced Marsh. The thinking simply did not possess the consistency of the past. It seemed as though Plan A had failed but there was no Plan B.

13 May 1972 • West Germany v England – Berlin
England: Banks, Hunter, Moore, McFarland, Hughes, Storey,
                      Madeley, Bell, Ball, Chivers, Marsh.[18]

England played a very physical game with very little flair. Netzer who had so lit up Wembley complained afterwards that the England players had "autographed" his legs. Those who followed Hunter and Storey week in, week out would have wryly smiled at the comment. This was always going to be the case from the moment the team was announced. A report in the *Telegraph* noted:

> "A great manager in his time, Ramsey was becoming increasingly erratic in his judgment. For the return leg he went to the other extreme, pairing Norman 'Bites yer legs' Hunter in midfield with Arsenal's uncompromising anchorman Peter Storey. A first-rate bad boy, Storey was once quoted as saying: 'If it wasn't for people like me, the Sugar Plum Fairy could play centre-forward.'" [19]

---

18   http://www.englandfc.com/MatchData/yearbyyear.
php?start=1970&end=1974&gender=M&level=FULL [online] [Accessed: March 2014].

19   Briggs, S. (2008) England v Germany at the Olympic Stadium: The Berlin Effect. *The Telegraph*. [Online] 18 November 2008. Available from: http://www.telegraph.co.uk/sport/football/teams/england/3479037/England-v-Germany-at-the-Olympic-Stadium-The-Berlin-Effect-Football.html [Accessed: 2 August 2014].

In his effort to avoid further embarrassment, Ramsey had only succeeded in appalling the Germans with his niggling, negative tactics.
As the *Welt Am Sonntag* correspondent put it, "England had betrayed
their own reputation for fair play".

Yes, Ramsey's thinking was confused but this also reflected
English football at the time. The English league possessed both the
hardest of footballers who took pride in their brutality – players such
as Norman Hunter, Peter Storey, Ron "chopper" Harris, and Tommy
Smith. The great Leeds team of the early 70s were renowned for their
toughness. At the other end of the scale, new players were emerging
that showed great skills that got the crowds to their feet – players
as Rodney Marsh, Kevin Keegan, Stan Bowles, Gerry Francis, Peter
Osgood, Alan Hudson, Ian Hutchinson, Tony Currie and Charlie
George. George Best had inspired a generation of new players along
from the 60s and English football arguably had one of its greatest
ever generations of skilled craftsmen – but along with the ultra physical. English football was "beauty and the beast" in character. It was
exciting and dramatic and as England manager, Ramsey has to pull
the two characters together to play as one. It was no easy challenge.

If one steps back, one can understand why Ramsey made the
decisions that he did. In Moore, Peters, Ball, Banks and until 1972,
Hurst – he had five players that transcended the norm and were
proven world-class players who could compete with the world's best.
The new breed of players coming through were increasingly physical
or maverick. Ramsey was looking was something deeper and better
but it was not as evident as it may appear. Players such as Storey and
Hunter may have saved England from further red faces in Berlin but
they were not going to win tournaments such the trusted five had.
Players such as Marsh, Osgood, and Hudson were mavericks, which
Ramsey struggled to accept. They could be brilliant one week and go

absent from games the next week. Ramsey wanted better. He needed world-class consistency, and needed to find the key to unlock the potential that was so clearly evident. It was not an easy puzzle to solve?

Ramsey was a conservative man of high morals and ethics and this new generation was posing him new questions and he needed to find the answers by the opening World Cup game in November.

"It could have been worse. Peters did dive to win a penalty. Thank God too. Otherwise we would have lost and our record in that group would have been; Won 1, Drawn 1, Lost 2. We weren't good enough".[20]

Paul (Supporter).

Focus group – London, March 2014.

3.

A System that Hindered Success

There has been much written about Sir Alf Ramsey, rightly so, as England's most successful manager, but very few knew Sir Alf. He was, in many ways, the ideal manager – private and one step removed from everyone. He knew his own mind, had courage and conviction and most importantly Sir Alf understood what it took to be an international player at the highest level. Many have written that Ramsey mistrusted flair. It has been said that he preferred a system over skill, but this is not borne out by the facts. The team that played Poland at Wembley was full of skilful players. No, it was more about the player – the man – and whether they were able to compete at the highest level, whether he could trust them to deliver. There are two amusing Jack Charlton stories over a response that Ramsey gave when Charlton asked why he had been selected in 66? The first response was:

> "Well, I choose the system and then the players that will suit that system. I do not always select the best players, Jack".

The second was:

> "I know that when Bobby Moore gets caught dribbling out of our box, you will be there to take no nonsense and clear the ball".

It was all about understanding the players and what they would contribute.

Ramsey understood three key factors:

1. He had little time with the players and therefore needed a clear structure that the players could understand easily and play to. English football was so competitive that it would be difficult to mould a team from players that wanted to beat each other each week and then come together ten times a year to play for the national team.

2. Success on the international stage required both great technique but also a special mentality. He was one of the first to understand that the mind was as important as the skill.

3. The player must have strength of character. The one thing that resonates about Ramsey's England players was that whether in triumph or defeat, there was a calmness about the players and structure. It is an old saying that says one learns most in moments of adversity and most were struck by the calm politeness of Ramsey in his darkest moment as the final whistle blew after the Poland match. He simply walked over to the Polish coach to shake this hand. After the West Germany defeat in 1970, England behaved with dignity despite the severe disappointment. If one looks at the pictures of the 66 triumph, the players look jubilant but not in any "over the top" way. Ramsey's way was about calm in either victory or defeat. It was – as trite as it may sound – about being a man.

Ramsey was a pragmatist who understood the International game far better than any other England manager. Sir Walter Winterbottom was a great coach, a technician but not a tough manager. Robson became a great manager but his great team of 1990 arguably came together through events rather than design, but he certainly understood players and the international game. The 1990 team was one of England's best ever and had grown together as a unit over six years through bad times (Euro 88) as well as the good. The team possessed a great goal scorer in Lineker; great flair players in Gascoigne, Waddle, Barnes, Platt and Beardsley and the "we will not give an inch" strength of Butcher, Shilton, Pearce and Mark Wright. With luck, they could have won the Italia 90.

Taylor and Revie had been great club managers and had wanted to translate what had been effective for them at club level to the international camp. This was never achievable and it showed a lack of understanding.

Greenwood was like Winterbottom in that he was a great coach and strategist. He led England back to being a competitive force and the 1982 team was very able. They struggled to ignite when it came to the big matches in the second stage but they were sound and at least England were back in the heart of world competition.

Venables, in 96, did build a potentially excellent team but outside factors did not allow him the opportunity to take it on. Hoddle too could have developed into a great manager but events off the football field led to his fall. Despite the Taylor years, England played some exceptional football during the 90s and possessed some great players.

On Erickson, the jury will always be out. Was he lucky in the players he had or was he, at the start at least, inspirational? Capello will not be remembered with fondness by many.

But Ramsey was an exceptional England manager who brought structure and understanding of what was needed in order to win at the highest levels. It can be argued that what became his Achilles heel in 1972 and 73, with his loyalty to his old guard, was because he could not find their replacements. Ramsey could not find players with the character and mental strength to be world-leading players and therefore, he stayed with those he knew had had it in the hope their abilities would not wane before he could find the next generation.

Of course the counter is that they were there in front of him but for some reason he did not seem to trust them. The Leeds team of the early 70s was loved and hated in equal measure. Loved may be too strong a word – they were certainly respected and hated in equal measure. They possessed some of the best players of the era but they were tough and uncompromising. However, that Leeds team possessed some able players that never really quite made it as Ramsey regulars. If one looks at the team of the 1973 FA Cup Final, it boasted English players such as Paul Reaney, Paul Madeley, Trevor Cherry, Mick Jones, Norman Hunter, and Allan Clarke. Only the last two were Ramsey regulars and both played less than 30 games for England – Hunter 28 times since his debut in the squad in 1965 and Clarke just 19 since his debut in 1970. Yes, Paul Madeley played against Poland and had become a regular but was still finding his feet.

In fairness, one could argue the same about Liverpool, who were battling a fierce contest with Leeds at the time. Liverpool had players also overlooked such as Tommy Smith, Chris Lawler, Larry Lloyd, Alex Lindsay, Ian Callaghan and Phil Thompson.

Arsenal – who had won the double in 71 – boasted in 1973 a team that included Charlie George, John Radford, Peter Storey, Peter Simpson, Bob McNab, George Armstrong, Alan Ball, Ray Kennedy, and Jeff Blockley. Only Ball was an established Ramsey regular and yet Arsenal came second in the league. Storey was in the squad and Kennedy would become a regular under Revie.

If one takes a step back and looks at the Leeds, Arsenal and Liverpool squads, the English players were good players at club level and were tough but the technique of those that lined up for England was higher. Who would have been selected from those teams above Roy McFarland or Bobby Moore? Who was better than Colin Bell, Tony Currie, Martin Peters? And who better than Chivers or Channon?

The truth just may lie in the fact that English football became so obsessed by defensive systems that it hindered the players of great technique thrive. Is it a coincidence that Bell, Currie, Peters, Chivers, McFarland, Shilton, and Channon all played for clubs outside of the top six in the English League?

It was once said by the great tennis player, John McEnroe that the difference in skill in the top 20 players in the world was marginal. What determined the difference lay in the mind. Two famous McEnroe quotes are:

"What is the single most important quality in a tennis champion? I would have to say desire, staying in there and winning matches when you are not playing that well."

"I think it's the mark of a great player to be confident in tough situations."[21]

Most top sportsmen would echo these words. Confidence is the major factor that lies between success and "might have been". The real point is about the inner confidence that you can win against the best opponents when the game is not going to plan. Top sportsmen will often talk about the importance of building a winning mentality when they have the inner belief they will win whatever the situation. And this lies at the heart of 73. Yes, England were unlucky, but are

21   Brainy Quote, (2014) http://www.brainyquote.com/quotes/authors/j/john_mcenroe.html [accessed: July 2014].

players that did not compete regularly and successfully at the highest levels of international competition really able to possess the inner belief and confidence that they can compete and win against the best.

In the 1972–73, English Championship – the season preceding the Poland match – Derby County (Roy McFarland) were seventh, Spurs (Peters and Chivers) eighth, Manchester City (Bell) 11th, Southampton (Channon) 13th, Sheffield United (Currie) 14th and Leicester City (Shilton) 16th.

So did we really expect an England team with eight players that were not used to winning consistently to possess a winning mentality at international level? Yes they were the best players but the confidence was understandably missing. Both Derby and Spurs had lost 13 games each in the 72–73 season. Manchester City had lost 16. Leicester had lost 15.

Liverpool had lost seven, Arsenal eight and Leeds 10. No one was a runaway winner and the fiercely competitive nature of the league was seen to make it one of the most exciting in the world and this was true. The crowds were passionate, tribal and hostile. The players were committed and gave everything. There was no quarter asked or given by any team.

But this in turn did not act as a breeding ground for success at international level. It did not build confidence and the systems employed by the best teams were designed to defend against great attacking players. It was also a gruelling long season with little rest for the players. Of course, the counter is that these are professional sportsmen who were privileged to be living their dreams. Very true and few of the players would argue against this – but it is missing the point.

The West German team that won the 1974 WC had five Bayern Munich players in the team. They had won their league in 1974, playing 34 matches in their league season, winning 20 and losing five. Of the West German team of 1974, all the players played in teams that came in the top five in the league – and Gunter Nezter who had destroyed England in 72 played for Real Madrid.

The team that won the most admirers in 1974 was the Dutch team with their "invention" of Total football, which would see the whole team attack. It was based around six players from the Ajax team and led by the greatest player in the world at the time, Johan Cruyff.

Cruyff looked physically frail but his technique was as good as any Brazilian from the team of 1970 and he had speed and agility to turn in the tightest of space and make life difficult for defenders. In the early 1970s, defensive systems and defenders dominated and it took players of real skill to unlock the defences. Cruyff could seemingly do it at will. He was the European Player of the Year in 1971, 1973 and 1974.

Ajax's midfield spread across the Dutch team with Keizer, Muhren, Hann and Neeskens. Neeskens was the playmaker who made the team tick and Haan the driving force from deep. In the 1978 World Cup, when the Dutch were in trouble, Haan would turn the course of matches with spectacular goals from 30 yards or more.

The Dutch coach, Rinus Michels, understood that at international level every small percentage created a winning margin and he focused on both skill plus physical conditioning. Michels led Ajax to three European Cups in the early 1970s and when Holland arrived in West Germany, they were the fittest and most technical team in the tournament. The 1974 Final was seen as West German efficiency over Dutch flair and craft.

The comparison is clear and easy. The England team of 1973 on that fateful night, against Poland, boasted a single player from the

Championship winning team – Emlyn Hughes – and only three from the top five teams. The Dutch team had six just from Ajax. The English team possessed players that could match anyone in the world and yet they were hindered before they even kicked a ball.

Arguably one of the most exciting and most naturally talented English teams of the era was Chelsea. Chelsea team was coached by Dave Sexton and boasted English players such as Peter Bonetti, Alan Hudson, John Hollins, Peter Osgood, Ian Hutchinson, Keith Weller, Peter Houseman, David Webb and Ron "chopper" Harris as well as the Scottish Internationals Eddie McCreddie and Charlie Cooke. Chelsea threatened to break through in the early 70s with this team winning the FA Cup in 1970 against Leeds United and the 1971 Cup Winners Cup against Real Madrid. Both finals were won after replays, which if anything, showed a fighting spirit to compete against the best. In talent terms alone, Keith Weller, Alan Hudson, Peter Osgood and Ian Hutchinson were good enough to have had successful England careers and all arguably should have been in or close to the 1973 England team.

So what happened?

Each has a different story but there is a theme:

Keith Weller left the Chelsea team after the 1971 victory over Real Madrid and transferred to Leicester City – a team not as talented or prominent. He did play for England four times but under Joe Mercer. Mercer was the interim manager before Revie and his team was deemed to have played some of the best football since 1970. If Mercer had stayed, Weller's England career may have flourished.

Alan Hudson played just twice for England – once in the victory over West Germany at Wembley in 75 and once in a 5–0 win over Cyprus. But Hudson suffered injuries and he clashed with Revie. He left Chelsea for Stoke City in 1974. Stoke at the time were a strong competitive outfit and Hudson then went to Arsenal in 76 but he never regained his England place.

Peter Osgood played only four times for England which was a surprise as he was one of England's most feared strikers and very talented. He was in the 1970 World Cup squad playing against Czechoslovakia and came on as a substitute against Romania. It was said that Ramsey disapproved of Osgood's lifestyle. Osgood left Chelsea, after a series of rows with Sexton also over his lifestyle for Southampton – another team lower in the league than Chelsea – where he did win the FA Cup in 1976.

Ian Hutchinson's career was blighted by injuries, including two broken legs, a broken arm, a broken toe and persistent knee trouble, which kept him out of the sides successful Cup Winners' Cup run the following year and limited him to just four appearances in the 1972–73 season. He retired in July 1976 aged 27, having been unable to conquer his injury woes. He made 144 appearances for Chelsea and scored 58 goals.

These were natural talents that were properly managed by the system and nurtured. In the 1972–73 season, this talented team's record in the league was average. They finished 12th, won just 13 games and lost 15 games. If Chelsea wanted to compete against the best, this was simply not a good enough return for the talent they had. The view was that the players had playboy lifestyles and this may have been true, but at the same time, the framework of the sport should have allowed such talents to flourish better.

Chelsea was not an isolated story. The West Ham squad of 72–73 boasted Moore, Brooking, plus the young talents of Billy Bonds, Geoff Pike, Frank Lamped Snr, Pop Robson and Tommy Taylor. Derby County had Kevin Hector – who could have become an England Striker – Roy MacFarland, Colin Todd, and David Nish. Nish and Todd were regarded as the two of the best young talents in the game.

Arguably the best run team on limited resources at the time was Ipswich Town under Bobby Robson and with Mick Mills as captain. Their best English players were the young Kevin Beattie, David Johnson (attack) and Brian Talbot. All three would go on to play for England but few would say they were as skilled as the Chelsea players. They were more functional and good team players.

Ipswich finished fourth in 72–73 with 17 victories and 11 defeats. If one compares the natural talent in the Chelsea team to that in the Ipswich team, the positions they both held in the league should have been reversed but this was the age when tactical systems and organization were dominant. Where England differed from their contemporaries in either Germany or Holland was that their best players invariably played in the best teams and their leagues were not as competitive, nor as physically draining.

In simple terms, England were at a disadvantage before they even stepped on the field and worse still the problems were not really understood nor cared about. Little would change for years to come, but England was defeating itself.

"It was typical of England. Great players but they weren't a team. They played like a collection of individuals who turned up for a match. This would be the same story until Greenwood got us going again in 1978. England wasted so much time and potential. If it had been a business, the directors would have been sacked but that's sport. If one looks at English sport, it seems as though we have the most players, and great characters, but there seemed little professionalism to nurture that into success unlike the Germans, Italian and Dutch who really understood what was needed. For years, it was said we were technically not as good as other teams but we possessed other qualities that other nations valued, such as our players would never give up and other countries did court our players such as Keegan. No, we just wasted time and talent. I wonder how much money was spent by average, lowly paid supporters following England during those years. They used their savings to support England. I wonder if the leadership were as committed to England?"

David (supporter).[22]

4.

ENGLAND HAD THE PLAYERS

The system may have been a hindrance to success at international level but the counter argument was that the domestic league was one of the most exciting in the world and attracted high audiences. England may have been a team in decline but football was still immensely popular.

It was full of passion, tension and English "blood and thunder". No team would give a quarter to another and any team on their day could win. One only has to look at the 1973 FA Cup Final when Second Division underdogs Sunderland beat firstly Arsenal in the semi-final (2–1) and then Leeds United in the Final. When a team from the second tier beats two of England's top three teams, how can one say that Sunderland were not worthy winners. Most will remember the game for a heart stopping save by Sunderland's goalkeeper Jim Montgomery from Peter Lorimer when the television commentators were already calling "goal" and for the genuine joy of the Sunderland manager, Bob Stokoe, as he raced to hug his Captain, Bobby Kerr. Both moments illustrated the drama and emotion of English football.

The players loved the atmosphere in the stadiums and the competitive nature of the league and cups. The fans loved it and arguably, in the period of economic difficulties, the game became an escape for many from reality of day-to-day life. Supporting one's team became almost tribal and the 70s saw the rise of English hooliganism. Stadiums became hotbeds for the alpha male. As one supporter once said; "Football allows me to pretend to be an intimidating warrior for two hours every week before I return to work" – Maurice, London focus group.

If one ever doubted the passion of the players and crowds, then one only has to study the season opening Charity Shield match in August 1974 at Wembley Stadium. There were close to 70,000 in the crowd to see Jack Taylor, the English referee who also refereed the 1974 World Cup Final, send off Kevin Keegan and Billy Bremner after a tussle between them. As they left the field, both men took off their shirts and threw them away in disgust. This was supposed to be a friendly match but there was no doubting the intensity.

Brazil had won the World Cup playing the "beautiful game" with stunning skill and great passing. English football was not for the softhearted. It was brutal with a set of fearsome defenders that took pride in their "no one will pass" mentality. This included Ron Harris, Jack Charlton, Willie Young, Gordon McQueen, Tommy Smith, Peter Storey, Frank McLintock, and of course, Norman Hunter.

And the gifted players thrived in this environment too. The 1970s saw a range of exceptional and skilful players grace the fields across England. The game may have become more organised and defensive but there were no shortage of great goal scorers and attackers. George Best led the way but was supported by Rodney Marsh, Francis Lee, Dennis Law, Stan Bowles, Martin Chivers, Charlie George, Joe Royle, Allan Clarke, Peter Osgood, Kevin Keegan, Trevor Francis, Mick Channon and Bob Latchford.

There were sparkling midfielders too – Tony Currie, Trevor Brooking, Peter Lorimer, Billy Bremner, Martin Peters, Alan Ball, Gerry Francis, Alan Hudson, Keith Weller, and Eddie Gray.

There were great players throughout the league in every position. In goal, there was Pat Jennings, Gordon Banks, Peter Shilton, Joe Corrigan, Gary Sprake, Ray Clemence and Peter Bonetti.

In defence, the hard men stepped forward with Bobby Moore, Roy McFarland, Colin Todd, Mike Pejic, Alec Lindsay, Tommy Smith, Mike England, Cyril Knowles, Dave Watson, Willie Young, Terry Cooper, Norman Hunter and Paul Madeley.

This was a golden era and in fairness the England team of 1973 possessed the potential to be a great team. This book may focus on England's failure but in the early 70s, the England team were putting poor teams to the sword. In the warm-up match for Poland, they easily beat Austria 7–0 with goals from Channon, Clarke (3), Bell, Chivers, and Currie. They looked comfortable, confident and ready for the big match coming up against Poland.

This team and players could have been formidable. They had come together as a team only in the six months before the fateful match against Poland and they were growing. One can put forward an argument that had they qualified, they would have developed further as a team and really challenged the best. One of the mistakes of the Revie era was that he broke up this England team too quickly.

Shilton was still emerging from the shadow of the great Gordon Banks. Banks had been a giant in the game and his tragic loss from the team following a car crash was bound to take time to replace. Many believe that if Banks had played against West Germany in 1970, England would have reached the Final. Many also believe that if England had not lost their dominant last line of defence, England would have qualified for the 74 World Cup. Banks was still world-class and still giving great performances. Shilton was an excellent goalkeeper but in truth, it takes a year to find one's feet at international level and Shilton was not quite ready for the Poland game. The shot that led to the Polish goal is one that he would have saved in nine in every 10 league games. It happens. Every developing player goes through the same learning curve – especially goalkeepers. Shilton would go on to become of the true England greats – only retiring after the final game of World Cup Italia 1990. However, during the Revie era, he was the understudy to Ray Clemence and only reclaimed the No One jersey as his own in 1982.

Similarly, Tony Currie was still in his first year of playing for England. He only played 17 times for England and yet he was one of the great midfielders of that time. He just did not have the time and opportunity to assert himself at the top level. He only played once for England under Revie and was recalled to the team by Ron Greenwood, but by then the best of Tony Currie was past. It is strange as Currie had joined Leeds in 1976 and went on to play some of his best football and yet Revie ignored his claims

Martin Chivers scored 13 goals in just 24 games and yet his career seemed to go into terminal decline after Poland 73. Chivers was the type of player that needed to feel confident and there has always been a view that he did not attack the Polish defence as he normally would do. Was he overawed by the occasion? Was it just one of those nights?

His record certainly suggests that he could have been a great goalscorer but something went wrong. He declined too early and quickly. The Poland match was his last for England and it seems, with his goalscoring record, nonsensical that he only played for England for two years – 1971–73. In fairness, Ramsey did not select Chivers after Poland for his final two matches and neither did Joe Mercer in his short tenure. It must have been a heavy blow to Chivers confidence and arguably an unfair one.

The 1975–76 season was Chivers' last at White Hart Lane as he struggled to find the net in a relatively poor Spurs team. He made 37 appearances in all competitions; scoring nine times, before joining Swiss club Servette for an £80,000 fee. In his eight and a half-year Spurs career, Chivers scored a total of 174 goals in 367 first team appearances and remained the leading Tottenham goalscorer in European competition for 39 years until he was overtaken by Jermain Defoe on 7 November 2013.

Mick Channon too was only a fledgling international but did survive under Revie to become one of the stalwarts of England during the mid 70s until Greenwood took over. Channon made his debut only in October 1972. Channon was a popular player with both fans and players as he was direct, scored goals and attacked defences. He was a good team man with a broader view of life. Football was not the be all and end all. His true passion was horse racing, which is where he would spend his later years training racehorses.

The key theme is that this England team was only just starting to come together and evolve. The Poland match was arguably six months to a year too early. The damage had been done in the 1–1 draw at Wembley against Wales and the defeat in Poland. If England had played to form in either of those two games, England would have been at the World Cup Finals in 74.

Most point to the 2–0 defeat in Poland as the low point, but truth is that it was the 1–1 draw at home to Wales with an England team that was unproven and containing players seeking to establish themselves at international level, but who would not even be in the team that played Poland. Ramsey had begun rebuilding after the European Nations Cup defeat to West Germany and it was simply too fast and England did not have the time for the natural development curve. The team that played Wales at Wembley contained Ray Clemence, Rodney Marsh, Kevin Keegan and Peter Storey. It still contained Alan Ball, Martin Peters, Bobby Moore, Norman Hunter, Colin Bell and Martin Chivers and should have – on paper – defeated Wales but Wales were tough competitors and contained highly experienced players in their line up such as Gary Sprake, Terry Yorath, Trevor

Hockey, Mike England, Leighton James and John Toshack. They were also playing their best football as a team and would go on to beat Poland 2–0 in March in Cardiff. The Wales team were, on their day, good opponents and England did not play to their potential, whilst Wales did.

Over the course of a few months, all expectations over how the qualifying group containing three teams would play out was turned on its head.

THE LEADING PLAYERS

Martin Peters – *Captain*

Martin Peters was the leading figure within the England set up in 1973 and rightly so. He was regarded as one of the most naturally talented footballers that England had ever produced and had been a World Cup winner – and scored in the Final – in 66. He had been a steadfast figure during the great days under Ramsey and during the rebuilding process.

When one looks back at the photographs and film from 1973, it does not capture the natural aura and presence of Martin Peters, that crowds across England saw each week. In 1972 and 73 he was probably the best player in England. He was not an aggressive player but he had vision and could change the course of a game in a single moment. He could play in the midfield, as a striker or on the wing. In October 1972, Peters' Tottenham team played at Old Trafford and won easily 4–1 with Peters scoring all four goals – he was the last man to score four goals against Manchester United.

Ramsey, after a game against Scotland in 1968, had described him as, "ten years ahead of his time," but in 1972–73, he was at his peak as an authoritative player and he could have gone to be one of the great players on the 74 World Cup stage along with Cruyff, Neeskens, Muller, Beckenbauer and Denya.

Peters was a relatively quietly spoken, modest man who led through his performances and actions. He was a natural successor as captain to his old friend and colleague, Bobby Moore. The two were similar in many ways. Both had come through the ranks with West Ham. Both led through their actions. Both were naturally gifted players and carried the respect of their teammates. Both possessed a winning mentality.

It seems strange – but illustrative of the problem – that instead of Peters leading England to respect in 74, his international career came to an abrupt end with the 2–0 defeat to Scotland at Hampden Park just prior to the World Cup Finals at the age of just 30. He had already been replaced as captain by Joe Mercer with Emlyn Hughes. A year earlier he was Captain Marvel and in May 1974, it was all over. He captained England just four times, during which time England had won once and drawn three times. He needed time to grow into the job. He had proven himself to be an exceptional leader at Tottenham and he could have been the same for England.

One should not shed too many tears. It may have been a disappointing end but Peters had a great career and will be always regarded as one of England's greatest.

Martin Peters had begun his career with West Ham in 1959, breaking into the first team on a regular basis in 1964. In 1965, he was a regular and part of West Ham's winning team of the European Cup Winners' Cup. His England career debuted in 1966 but with West Ham he was always the junior of the Moore, Hurst, Peters trio. Moore and Hurst would not see Peters in that way, but they were the more commanding figures at the club and Peters did sit in their shadows. A move away from West Ham was sensible for his own development and in March 1970, he joined Tottenham Hotspur where he really did flourish as his own man and then as captain. He played for Tottenham for five years and in that time won two League Cups, the UEFA Cup against Wolves in 72 and played in an UEFA Cup Final against Feyenoord, which was lost 2–0. He made 189 appearances for Spurs, scoring 49 goals, in what was a successful period.

In March 1975, with his England career over and 31 years old, Peters transferred to Norwich City where he went on to play 206 matches scoring 46 goals. He helped establish Norwich City as a true First Division club. He was their player of the year two years in a row in 1976 and 1977 and played for them up to 1980.

Just maybe England forgot about their captain too quickly? In 1970 he had transferred at a record breaking £200,000 to Spurs. In 1975, he was transferred to Norwich for just £50,000.

One cannot say that a man who was part of the World Cup Winning team, who captained his country and won 67 caps did not fully realise his potential, but there was more that could have come from Peters at the highest level. Ramsey recognised the value of the man and player and if things had been different against Poland, the chances are that Peters would have become recognised as one England's best captains as well as players. But that is life – it can cruelly move on – and Revie needed to rebuild England and wanted a new leader.

Emlyn Hughes – *Left-back*
Emlyn Hughes was a key figure for England during the 1970s. When one talks of the many great talents within England's set up in 1973, Hughes would not jump off the tongue as one of the leading names, but he was all about courage, strength and positivity. He was the kind of character that one would want in a team with you – never

beaten, always positive, He was one of the great Liverpool defence in the final Shankly years and would remain with Liverpool through two European Cup triumphs in 1977 and 1978; leaving only in 1979, playing 474 games for Liverpool.

To illustrate the importance of Hughes within the England set up, he was appointed Captain by the interim manager Joe Mercer and led out the team for the first time against Wales in May 1974. He went on to captain England for all Mercer's seven matches in charge and England were viewed to have played some of the best football for some time on their European tour.

He retained the role for the first two of Revie's matches but then was surprisingly dropped from the team as Revie turned to Alan Ball. He spent a year in the wilderness before he returned for the World Cup qualifiers and played in the tactically poor 2–0 defeat to Italy. He returned to the captaincy briefly in 1977 when Kevin Keegan was injured, but became the captain again under Greenwood. He captained England for the last time in 1980 in a 1–1 draw with Northern Ireland and played his last game against Scotland in the next game. He played 62 times for England.

Hughes was not the most skilful player, but he was all about heart. He would never give up as was shown by the number of times England turned to him to be their captain. He even played and captained a Liverpool team when there was personal anger and bitterness between Hughes and Tommy Smith. Whatever the rights and wrongs of the situation, the idea of two of a team's back four not even being on speaking terms would be disastrous for a team, but it says much for both men that they played together for seven years after their fallout and Liverpool never suffered as a result. Both were ultimate competitors who put Liverpool before themselves.

Colin Bell – *Midfielder*

In 1973, Colin Bell was coming to his peak. He was the successor to the great Bobby Charlton in the England team and had huge energy and drive. In the eyes of many he played his finest game for England in the 7–0 defeat of Austria just before the Poland match. Charlton had been a dominant figure for England and it was always felt that Charlton's substitution with Bell was the cause of England's defeat in the 1970 quarter-final, as it gave the West German's the confidence to take more risks as they attacked. Bell was undeterred by any negativity – he took his chance and made the position his own for England and he was desperately upset by England's failure in 73.

Under Revie, Bell went onto to play some exceptional football, but unfortunately was injured in a league match against Manchester United and he would never be the same player again. He played 48 times for England and scored nine goals.

Norman Hunter – *Defender*

Norman Hunter was known as a tough no nonsense player. Known for his tackling, he was nicknamed "Bites Yer Legs" Hunter. The nickname originated from a banner held up by Leeds United fans at the 1972 FA Cup Final against Arsenal; the banner simply read "Norman bites yer legs". When Hunter himself suffered a broken leg, club trainer <u>Les Cocker</u> was informed that, "Hunter had broken a leg" and responded with, "whose is it?"

It was then one of life's great ironies that it would be Hunter's missed tackle that would lead to Poland's goal at Wembley.

It is too easy to suggest that Hunter had recently taken over from Moore and was trying to prove himself, but the truth is that Hunter had been in the England set up for a long time. He made his debut in 1965, was in the 1966 England squad and even scored the winning goal in the 1968 European Championships quarter-final match against Spain. However he only played 28 games for England and his final game was in 1974. Many blamed him for the draw with Poland, which was harsh and many never expected Revie to select him for England. But Hunter's England career did not last much longer.

Allan Clarke – *Striker*

Allan Clarke was one of the best strikers in England between 1968 and 1975. He was a very skilful player whose record as a goalscorer was excellent. He scored 110 goals for Leeds United in 273 games and 10 goals for England in just 19 matches – he even scored on his England debut in the 1970 World Cup Finals in the 1–0 win over Czechoslovakia.

Clarke looked perfectly suited to the pressures of international football and it was strange that he was nurtured and developed better by Ramsey between 1970 and 73. True, Clarke was competing against a number of great strikers and seemed to be the understudy for Hurst and Chivers at first and then when Hurst was dropped, Ramsey experimented with Joe Royle, Mick Channon and Malcolm Macdonald. Clarke was recalled for the 5–0 win over Scotland in February 1973 but he needed longer. Royle and MacDonald were traditional tough English centre-forwards. Clarke was more subtle and had guile – qualities that were more suited to the international arena than the traditional approach that international teams had learnt how to combat. Revie too went with the traditional approach and with MacDonald but the best teams in the world easily handled such players. Clarke should have been given more opportunities. His record of 10 goals in 19 matches makes its own statement. Clarke often saved his best performances for the big occasion. His place in domestic history was secured with his diving header to win the 1972

Centenary FA Cup Final against Arsenal. He was also a consistent force for Leeds United on the European stage and gave the Bayern Munich defence a torrid time in the first half of the 1975 European Cup Final.

There is no doubt that England possessed the players to have graced the World Cup Finals in 1974. For many the Poland match marked the finals days of their international careers and this included talent that should have been kept faith with and nurtured far better. This was a still young, even inexperienced team, which had a setback. The real failure was how this team was broken up.

"All I remember is feeling really sad and disappointed. It was weird. I didn't feel let down by the players but I did feel England had let down the world game, as we should have been competing in the World Cup. I couldn't understand how we had fallen so far so quickly. I was still young but all I had heard about was how good we were and how good our players were; that we had the best league in the world and that everyone loved to try and beat England. And now we could not even qualify. For a young teenager, this was all very hard to put into context. Were we good enough or weren't we?"

Andrew (Supporter).[23]

23   London Focus group February 2014.

5.

Poland - Where Did They Come From?

The story has, so far, been dominated from the English perspective but of course, it is equally important to view the events from the Polish perspective.

Was it really just English error and misfortune or were the Polish, in truth, a far better team than the "We murdered them" headlines in the English newspapers gave credit for?

How did Poland turn their fortunes around from being a team easily defeated by Wales – 2–0 – in the first match of qualifying to come third in the 1974 Finals, defeating the mighty Brazil in the process. It was quite a journey. In 1973, Brazil were the undisputed champions who the world looked to as the benchmark. Wales were a team that had not quaffed for the Finals since 1958 and were in the second tier of European football, let alone world soccer. We can write whatever we wish about the failure of England, but the achievements of this Polish team to grow and evolve as an international force was an extraordinary story, which would have required great substance and character.

The most renowned Polish team was the one of this period, in West Germany in 1974, they defeated Brazil 1–0 to claim third place in the tournament, with striker Grzegorz Lato winning the Golden Boot for his seven goals. This was the start of a golden period for the international team and Poland also finished third in the 1982 beating France 3–2 in the third-place play-off.

So where does their story start?

Poland was a mostly unknown force on the international foot-

<u>ball</u> scene before their exploit in 1973 and 1974. However, the signs were evident that this team could compete as the core of the team successfully achieved a gold medal place in the Munich Olympics in 1972. The Olympics were not considered a major tournament by most western nations, but eastern European countries bypassed the amateur rules by fielding their full national teams, as most players also had employment with national industries or within the army. However, they sparkled at the Olympics with their lightning speed and incredible team spirit, defeating Hungary in the Final. Hungary had been the 1964 and 1968 Olympic Champions.

Poland were coached by Kazimierz Górski, who also managed the Polish national team. With future stars like Grzegorz Lato, the Poles were considered to be the best team of the tournament. In the Final, they trailed Hungary at half-time, but two goals by Kazimierz Deyna turned the match around. Two years later, Górski was the man who would lead the Polish team to a third place at the World Cup – also in West Germany – with many of the players that took the gold medal in München. Lato and Denya became football icons in 74 but the basis of their success lay with the 1972 triumph. It gave them a confidence that they could compete successfully and breed a winning mentality.

In the first round of the competition, Poland qualified with three straight wins:

- 5–1 v Colombia
- 4–0 v Ghana
- 2–1 v East Germany[24]
- In the second round, they won two more games and drew to qualify for the Final:

---

24   http://en.wikipedia.org/wiki/Poland_national_football_team [online accessed: June 2014].

- 1–1 v Denmark
- 2–1 v Soviet Union
- 5–0 v Morocco[25]

They won the final 2–1 against Hungary. Their record was:

W6 D1 L0 GF 21 GA 5

More importantly, they had proved to themselves that they were a good team by defeating strong teams in East Germany and the Soviet Union as well as Hungary.

Yes, in qualifying, Poland surprised world football by eliminating England, but the success they had shown on the amateur world stage moved onto the professional arena. This was an exceptional team. They had maybe the one quality England lacked in 1973 – confidence to win.

In their opening match of Germany 74 Poland met Argentina, a team that was appearing in their sixth World Cup. Within eight minutes Poland were up 2–0, Grzegorz Lato opened the scoring in the seventh minute and just a minute later Andrzej Szarmach doubled the lead. In the 60th minute Argentina cut the lead in half when Ramon Heredia scored. But two minutes later Lato got his second, which turned out to be the winning goal as Carlos Babington gave Argentina their second in the 66th. The match finished 3–2 to Poland.

Poland easily beat the Caribbean nation of Haiti 7–0 in their second game. The goals included a hat-trick from Szarmach and two from Lato. In their final match of the first stage Poland met Italy, who were second at the previous World Cup in 1970. Poland were already

25   http://en.wikipedia.org/wiki/Poland_national_football_team [online accessed: June 2014].

through to the second round but needed at least a tie to win the group. At half-time Poland was leading 2–0 with goals from Andrzej Szarmach and Kazimierz Deyna. It was not until the 86th minute that Italy managed a consolation goal through Fabio Capello. This gave Poland their third consecutive win, which led them to win the group. In the second round Poland first won 1–0 against a Swedish side, which had not let in any goals in their first three matches. Lato scored the only goal of the game. Next was Yugoslavia who had drawn with Brazil and Scotland and won 9–0 against Zaire in the first round. Poland were awarded a penalty in the 24th minute and took the lead when Deyna converted. Stanislav Karasi tied it up for Yugoslavia in the 43rd. Lato won it for Poland again when he scored in the 62nd making the final score 2–1 in Poland's favour.

On 3 July, 1974 came the game that could have sent Poland into the 1974 FIFA World Cup Final. They played against the eventual champions West Germany. It had rained all day long, the field was entirely flooded. Poland wanted the game postponed but the Austrian referee would not agree. The game went ahead. Poland needed a win to be in the Final, a draw was enough for the Germans. But in the miserably wet conditions Poland's speed was of no use, since the ball would not roll like it does on a dry field. Gerd Müller scored the winning goal in the 76th minute for Germany. The romantic story of the Polish underdogs shocking the world had come to a halt.

Poland would end the amazing run with a 1–0 victory over Brazil in the third place game. Lato scored the winning goal his seventh of the tournament crowning him the top scorer of the World Cup.

So maybe England were simply beaten by a team on the rise and they were not ready for the challenge?

Jan Tomaszewski made some interesting comments in an interview made forty years later:

"I remember that day alongside the victory we achieved over England in Chorzow on 6 June. We had lost against Wales in Cardiff and England arrived with their strongest possible squad, which included world champions such as Bobby Moore and Martin Peters and a bunch of the best footballers in the world. It was like England came to Poland with the sole aim of fulfilling their duty of advancing to the World Cup. But Kazimierz Gorski prepared us with great tactics: he told us we had to go to battle, which we didn't do in Wales. Before the game the mood was that we had lost the opportunity to play in the finals, but afterwards we knew it could still happen. We played on the borderline in terms of fouling: it wasn't brutal though, it was a fair fight, and it was Alan Ball that was shown a red card, not Leslaw Cmikiewicz (who had fouled Peters prior to the sending-off)."

"After that we beat Wales 3–0 and then came the match at Wembley – we needed a draw and England had to win. We knew we could get a result, even in a great atmospheric stadium like Wembley – not many of us had played in such a place. The genius Gorski said that we needed to slow the game and keep the ball as much as possible, because when England had the ball, the crowd was so loud that we couldn't hear ourselves think – it was hard to communicate with my defence. Whenever I went for the ball my team-mates covered the goalline behind me – I made a lot of mistakes but they were fixed by Gorski's tactics. When you play for your country, by the 70th minute of the match your body is exhausted, but you can give more from the heart. And we did that. I think it was the happiest day in Polish football history."

"What more can I say? We proved that football is a game of coincidence and that sometimes theoretically weaker teams can beat better ones, because it was a winning draw. And I said afterwards that those who had survived Wembley could go to the World Cup with their heads held high – and we went on to prove it [by finishing third in Germany]."

"For me, the title 'The man who stopped England' is true – but in the sense that that man consisted of 12 parts: Gorski and 11 players, who he knew how to organise on the pitch. Of course it's a big pleasure for me to be talked about in that way and I am thankful for such a nickname, but football is a team sport. It works both ways: after we lost to the Germans 3–1 on my debut in 1971 I was the most unpopular man in Poland: half of the country wanted to hang me and the other half to send me into exile. So it was nice to be singled out again in a positive way by the English press."

What did you think when you heard that Brian Clough had described you as a clown prior to the Wembley match?

"It's a psychological battle: he had the power to say that Englishmen were better than the rest because they had recently been world champions. The entire football world also thought like that about the English. Such psychology remains common in football today. You have to be resilient: I was resilient back then, and my colleagues were too. England had beaten Austria 7–0 and we were similar to Austria in terms of ability. Honestly, when I was listening to the national anthems in front of the English team and the royal box, I thought:

'God, I hope we don't become another Austria here.' England had the best footballers in the world."

What happened with your hand injury?

"At the start of the match I was so nervous that I dropped the ball and didn't notice Allan Clarke standing two metres away from me. He jumped for the ball and I somehow managed to cover it, but he hit me in the hand. It wasn't deliberate – I would do the same if I was trying to score. My hand was frozen after that and I played with it until the end of the match. The first comment from my team-mate Adam Musial after the game was: 'It's good that he kicked you.' I said: 'Why?' And he answered: 'Because he woke you up!'"

How was the result received in Poland?

"In Poland it was hailed as a miracle, to match when we stopped the Bolsheviks in 1920. It was a euphoric reception."[26]

One can understand Poland's joy but the facts do say that they deserved it. If one look at their results in the run up to the game they were clearly playing confident good football.

15 Oct 1972	Poland v Czechoslovakia	**W 3–0**	**International**
20 Mar 1973	Poland v USA	**W 4–0**	**International**
28 Mar 1973	Wales v Poland	**L 2–0**	**FIFA World Cup**

---

26   Eurosport. (2012) *Tomaszewski exclusive: England 'miracle' in 1973 like beating Bolsheviks.* [Online] Available from: http://au.eurosport.com/football/world-cup/2018/england-v-poland-classic-matches_sto3459419/story.shtml [Accessed: 23 September 2014].

13 May 1973	Poland v Yugoslavia	D 2–2	International
16 May 1973	Poland v Rep of Ireland	W 2–0	International
06 Jun 1973	Poland v England	W 2–0	FIFA World Cup
01 Aug 1973	Canada v Poland	W 1–3	International
03 Aug 1973	USA v Poland	W 0–1	International
05 Aug 1973	Mexico v Poland	W 0–1	International
08 Aug 1973	Mexico v Poland	W 1–2	International
10 Aug 1973	USA v Poland	W 0–4	International
12 Aug 1973	USA v Poland	L 1–0	International
19 Aug 1973	Bulgaria v Poland	W 0–2	International
26 Sep 1973	Poland v Wales	W 3–0	FIFA World Cup
10 Oct 1973	Netherlands v Poland	D 1-1	International
17 Oct 1973	England v Poland	D 1–1	FIFA World Cup

And into 1974, this continued:

15 Apr 1974	Haiti v Poland	W 1–3	International
17 Apr 1974	Belgium v Poland	D 1–1	International
15 May 1974	Poland v Greece	W 2–0	International
15 Jun 1974	Argentina v Poland	W 2–3	FIFA World Cup
19 Jun 1974	Haiti v Poland	W 0-7	FIFA World Cup
23 Jun 1974	Italy v Poland	W 1–2	FIFA World Cup
26 Jun 1974	Poland v Sweden	W 1–0	FIFA World Cup
30 Jun 1974	Poland v Yugoslavia	W 2–1	FIFA World Cup
03 Jul 1974	West Germany v Poland	L 1–0	FIFA World Cup[1]

Now compare to England's results in the lead up to the match:

Nov 1972	**Wales v England**	W 0–1	FIFA World Cup
24 Jan 1973	**England v Wales**	D 1–1	FIFA World Cup
14 Feb 1973	**Scotland v England**	W0–5	Scottish FA 100th Anniv
12 May 1973	**N Ireland v England**	W 1–2	Home Championship

15 May 1973	England v Wales	W 3–0	Home Championship
19 May 1973	England v Scotland	W 1–0	Home Championship
27 May 1973	Czechoslovakia v England	D 1–1	International
6 June 1973	Poland v England	L 2–0	FIFA World Cup
10 June 1973	Russia v England	W 1–2	International
14 June 1973	Italy v England	L 2–0	International[27]
24 Sept 1973	England v Austria	W 7–0	International

Poland were playing the better, more confident football from 1972 through to and beyond the match. They had gained confidence in winning an International tournament and then they let that belief grow during the rest of 1972 and into 1973 and 1974. They were a strong confident team and England were struggling to find their right combinations. England were still a strong footballing power but they did not have a team.

The most telling image from 17 October 1973 was not any move or moment in the actual match but as the teams lined up for the National anthems. England looked like strangers – a collection of individuals thrown together. They stood part and showed no unity. England had lost before a ball had been kicked and probably Poland deserved to qualify and enjoy the success that they had. This does not mean England could not have gone on to achieve great feats, but Poland were the better team in 1973. They were on the rise and this was their moment in time.

The fact that England dominated them at Wembley makes two telling points:

1. The respect that England still possessed combined with the aura of Wembley.

27   http://www.englandfc.com/MatchData/yearbyyear.
php?start=1970&end=1974&gender=M&level=FULL (accessed: June 2014).

2. This England team could have evolved into a very strong team.

But history has shown us that sport is cruel and has little time for romantic tales or pity. England's history and potential counted for nothing and Poland deservedly took their place in the Finals. They beat England in Poland. They had beaten Wales comprehensively too. They beat Mexico twice in the summer plus Bulgaria way and most importantly they drew 1–1 with the most technically talented team in the world – Holland – a week before they came to Wembley.

Their record over the year was superior to England's and they had proven themselves as worthy competitors – yet they still feared England.

POLAND – THE LEAD CHARACTERS

Kazimierz Górski – *The Coach*

Gorski came through the ranks of management with the Polish international side. He began his career as a coach of Polish national junior team from 1956 to 1966, Polish U-23 national team from 1966 to 1970, and finally the first Poland national football team from 1970 to 1976. His first international match was held on 5 May 1971 in Lausanne against Switzerland. His major successes were winning the gold medal in the 1972 Olympic Games in Munich; third place in the 1974 World Cup held in Germany; and another silver medal for second place in the 1976 Olympic Games in Montreal. Kazimierz Górski was the coach for the Polish national team in 73 matches (with 45 wins).

After resigning his position in Polish national team, he went to Greece and was a successful coach of Panathinaikos Athens, Kastoria FC, Olympiakos Piraeus and Ethnikos Piraeus.

Gorski was the father of Poland's Golden era. He may have had the players of natural talent but he instilled in them a belief that they could compete. Poland had been through years of underachievement. Their history is littered with players of great ability but they had never before had such a strong team. Gorski nurtured them through setbacks to become a force. One should not overlook how the result in their opening match against Poland must have set back Gorski and his plans. A 2–0 defeat against Wales was far from a result that would be deemed likely less than 18 month later but Gorski kept his nerve, took the defeat and did let his players feel they could still not turn events around and succeed.

Most International teams are built over years. Poland came from nowhere and in two years became one of the top sides in the world.

Grzegorz Lato

He was the leading scorer at the 1974 World Cup. Lato's playing career coincided with the golden era of Polish football, which began with Olympic gold in Munich in 1972 and ended a decade later with third place at the 1982 World Cup in Spain, a repeat of the Poles' impressive finish in 1974 in Germany. He is the only Polish player ever to win the Golden boot at a World Cup.

For Poland, Lato has been capped a record 104 times between 1971 and 1984; he scored 45 goals, which is second best in national history behind Włodzimierz Lubański. Other than the 1974 World Cup, where he scored seven goals, he also participated in the 1978 and 1982 tournaments. In the 1974 World Cup, he won the Golden Shoe after scoring 7 goals throughout the tournament. The real change in opinion over Poland came in the match in the group stages defeating Argentina by a score of 3–2, with two goals from Lato, the first being scored after just seven minutes of play.

Confidence grew a and feeling of momentum, Poland then posted the tournament's second largest win with a 7–0 defeat of Haiti (the largest being Yugoslavia's 9–0 demolition of Zaire), with Lato weighing in with another two strikes. In the second round, the Stal Mielec-based striker was even more instrumental, scoring winning goals against Group B rivals Sweden (1–0) and Yugoslavia (2–1). And while even Lato was powerless to prevent an agonising 1–0 defeat by Germany in Frankfurt, the in-form marksman was able to propel his team to third place courtesy of the only goal in the play-off victory over Brazil. He was then known as Poland's favourite player. While playing for Poland, he helped them win several titles.

Kazimierz Deyna – *Captain*

On 24 April 1968, Deyna made his debut for Poland in a match against Turkey in Chorzów. Together with his team he won the gold medal in the 1972 Summer Olympics in Munich, and the bronze in Football World Cup 1974, after a match against Brazil.

In 1972 he was also the top goalscorer of the Olympic Games, with a total of nine goals. In the 1976 Summer Olympics his team yet again reached the finals and won the silver medal. Additionally, he was ranked third in the European Footballer of the Year for 1974, behind Johann Cruyff and Franz Beckenbauer respectively.

Deyna played for Poland on 97 (84 after the deduction of Olympic Football Tournament competition games) occasions, scoring 41 goals, and often captained the side. He had the ability to score from unusual positions, e.g. directly from a corner. Thanks to his skills, he was chosen several times as *Football Player of the Year* by Polish fans. In 1978 he captained Poland at the FIFA World Cup in Argentina, where the team reached the second phase.

Soon afterwards Deyna was transferred to English club Manchester City FC, making his debut in November 1978, and being one of the first wave of overseas players to play in the English league. His time in England was marred by a series of injuries, and he left in January 1981, shortly after a change in team manager, having made only 43 appearances in all competitions. However, he was regarded as an exceptionally gifted playmaker and became a cult figure with City fans. Deyna scored thirteen goals in his time with the club. Furthermore, his seven goals in the last eight games of the 1978–79 season were crucial for Manchester City avoiding relegation.

Jan Tomaszewski

As a footballer, he was nicknamed "Tomek" and "The Man That Stopped England", and was named Best Goalkeeper in the 1974 World Cup. Brian Clough had famously dubbed Tomaszewski a "Clown" before the match but this was just another example of the English not understanding who they were playing. Tomaszewski was a fine 'keeper.

"He hurled himself arms, knees and bumps-a-daisy all over his penalty area like a slackly strung marionette", Frank Keating wrote In *The Guardian*. "And all with a half-taunting, half-surprised smile which made one think this might be his first-ever game". England's Mick Channon said of the match, "We were criticized for not being more patient. How can you be more patient? We had complete control of the game, constantly shooting on their goal, what difference would it make? Just one of those days when it won't go in. If it had been any other game, if the result hadn't been so crucial, you'd have been happy with the performance!"[28]

---

28   Channel 4. (2013) England v Poland at Wembley – ITN archive (1973). [Online] Available from: http://www.channel4.com/news/poland-england-wembley-world-cup-1973-tomaszewski [Accessed: 19 November 2014].

"In the event, despite England dominating the match and having 35 shots on goal, Tomaszewski played the game of his life, keeping out everything the 'fast English forwards' could throw at him. A 1–1 draw saw the Poles through to the 1974 World Cup in West Germany at England's expense."[29]

(ITN Archive).

29   Channel 4. (2013) England v Poland at Wembley – ITN archive (1973). [Online] Available from: http://www.channel4.com/news/poland-england-wembley-world-cup-1973-tomaszewski [Accessed: 19 November 2014].

6.

17 OCTOBER - THE EMOTION AND DESPAIR

The build up to the match was both nervous and tense. This was arguably England's most important match for many years, maybe since 1953, as for the first time since they were destroyed by the Hungarians at Wembley, their standing as a world power was under serious questioning. Their decline had been dramatic. They had won the World Cup just seven years earlier and three years earlier had been many observers favourites to reach the Final.

As has been discussed, England were spluttering as a team and their form in qualifying had been poor. Poland in contrast were a growing team but this had not been fully recognised within England. Brian Clough famously dismissed Tomaszewski as a "clown" and Peter Taylor had called Poland "Donkeys". Both were arrogant, ill-considered comments. As is the way with life, when so much arrogance exists a fall is normally close by. The majority of the 100,000 that filled Wembley that fateful night still expected England to prevail

However, if one watches the England team that night, it appeared as though that they did not share this arrogance. As they walked out behind Martin Peters they looked nervous and disconnected from each other. They looked like a collection of individuals rather than a team. Poland in contrast looked like a well-drilled unit. Poland were ready for the battle ahead.

Before the match, Polish coach Kazimierz Górski told his players, "You can play football for 20 years and play 1,000 times for the national team and nobody will remember you. But tonight, in one game, you have the chance to put your names in the history books."

For the Polish players, this was their Cup Final. They were playing for their country and for history. There would be no shame in losing to England. For England, there was fear in their body language. These were hardened players but the tension was clearly evident.

It is the contradictions and questions that make this match so intriguing and fascinating. England were the former World Champions who looked ill at ease. And yet once play began they dominated the match with 35 shots on goal. In most matches one would expect 35 shots to be rewarded with at least three goals – on the ratio of one in 11. They had been nervous and disconnected but the collection of individuals played some sparkling and exciting football and Poland stayed in the match with a mix of a "game of a lifetime" from Tomaszewski, some desperate defending, some luck and maybe some lack of conviction in England's finishing which meant the shots were not quite as powerful or accurate as they would have been for their clubs. England's solitary goal came from a soft penalty when, in truth, England's captain dived to win the award. How can a game that was so dominated really come down to a dive to win a goal?

The answer may lie in confidence. England's team possessed an attacking force that was the finest of the English league. These were players that excited crowds with heroics week, week out. So what happened?

If one watches the game, it was England's midfield that were the dominant force – Peters, Currie and Bell – and they dictated the match. They played some superb football and they were ably supported by Channon on the outside plus a defence that was ready to attack in Hughes, Hunter, McFarland and Madeley. The three players that took the most of the criticism in the aftermath of the match were Shilton, Hunter and Chivers. Yes, Shilton and Hunter made mistakes but football is about mistakes. Mistakes happen; if they didn't there would be no goals and yes, one mistake led to a Polish goal. But England should still have prevailed.

This does not mean that Chivers and Clarke should take the blame. Yes this was Chivers poorest game and he probably was not experienced enough as an international to really enforce his authority on the match, but Poland packed the defence and relied on last-ditch heroics.

So what did go wrong?

It may be as simple as some of England's players being defeated by a mix of nerves, tension and inexperience. England possessed – for a supposed great footballing power – a relatively inexperienced team. Beyond Peters and Bell, few of the players had played more than 20 times for England. It is often said that it will take two years before a player will feel at ease as an international. The reality was that England were still in their infancy as a team. England had become a second tier world power after the 1–3 defeat against West Germany in 72 and in eighteen months the new team had great promise, but were not yet the finished article. On top of this, nerves sap the energy and power from the legs and this affected a few of the players, plus Poland were a team that had won Olympic Gold and had belief.

The counter arguments are:

- The Olympics were for amateurs and not of the same level as full internationals. There was no comparison. A fair argument but three points:
    - One only has to look at how Olympic Gold (London 2012) clearly increased Andy Murray's confidence to

win at Wimbledon, which he did in the following year (2013). It has a psychological affect from winning an international competition. Poland had won a major competition in 1972. The last England had won was in 66.

○ Poland did defeat three major East European teams in Hungary, Soviet Union and East Germany on their way to the Olympic title. All the East European International teams were amateurs. The Soviet Union had reached the Final of the European Nations Cup in 72. East Germany beat West Germany in the World Cup in 74 and was seen to be one of the outside bets for the World Cup in 74.

- This was England with the finest league in the world. They should naturally prevail and win through. A simplistic argument. It takes time for international teams to grow and become real forces. One only has to look at the Sir Clive Woodward story with the England Rugby Union team. The team that won the World Cup had no few moments of adversity and defeat on the way to their triumph. The journey to confidence takes time and often comes from adversity. The England team of 73 could – with time – have grown to be as a good as the team of 66 or 70 if the authorities and manager had kept faith with the team and players.

England played with an inexperienced team against what was a growing football force enjoying their golden era. England still played some exceptional football and possessed some great players. All one can say is that Ramsey should have started rebuilding soon after the 70 World Cup but even if this was true, he was unlucky to lose Gordon

Banks. Gordon Banks had been one of the cornerstones of the great England team. Maybe too much rested on his shoulders. They lost to West Germany in 70 to goals that Banks would most probably have saved. Bonetti was a great 'keeper but he was at fault in that match. Maybe through nerves and inexperience? In 71 and, Banks – like Peters – was playing some superb football. Stoke were enjoying their greatest period with Banks as their last line of defence. Few forget his penalty save from Geoff Hurst in the 72 League Cup and a few months later, Stoke won their first Cup Final v Chelsea at Wembley. In the FA Cup semi-finals, Stoke and Arsenal fought fierce encounters and Banks was at his best. He seemed to be growing with each passing year. In October 1972, Banks had hurt in a car crash; losing the sight of one eye. Many fans of that era still remember exactly where they were when they heard the news of Bank's accident. It was that important and he was that important to England. If he had played against Poland, the chances are high that he would have saved the shot from Domarski. Shilton would have saved it nine times out of 10 but he just didn't on that day, probably because he was trying to make a perfect save rather than just parry it away.

Some argue that Ramsey distrusted natural flair and liked organised systems. His teams were certainly very disciplined, organised and tactically astute but in 73, he selected the best players with those with great flair and talent.

Time had run out on England. As the whistle blew Ramsey was the epitome of grace and dignity in defeat. He must have felt deeply hurt for he was a proud man, but one couldn't tell as he walked across to the Polish coach, calmly shook his hand and then walked off into the night. Ramsey showed himself in that moment as the man and champion that he was – England's finest, even at the worst moment.

40 years later, as England again met Poland at Wembley in a World Cup Qualifier many of the players opened up to their hurt they had felt back in the 1973.

"It was the lowest point of my England career."

"I've never even seen the game. Why would I want to? Too many bad memories."

"I think it was the most disappointed I ever was, not only for the players but for Sir Alf Ramsey as well. It hurt him tremendously."[30]
  Martin Peters

"I will never forget the feeling of devastation after the draw against Poland in 1973. The dressing room was like a morgue with a lot of the players crying, sank to their knees."

"We had missed a massive chance to play at the <u>World Cup</u> and for many players it was their last chance gone. It was my first opportunity to play in the competition and luckily I went on to play in three of them after 1974 but for some people, like Norman Hunter and Allan Clarke, it was something they would never be able to achieve again. The enormity of what happened really hit home for me when we were watching the World Cup on television."

---

30   *Daily Star.* (2013) *Martin Peters warns England: Don't blow it like we did!* [Online] Available from: http://www.dailystar.co.uk/sport/football/345141/ Martin-Peters-warns-England-Don-t-blow-it-like-we-did [Accessed: 3 September 2014].

"Sir Alf Ramsey also left as manager shortly afterwards and the image of him walking towards the tunnel has been replayed over and over again."

"It was one of those nights that has gone down in history. We were expected to roll them over but their goal was their only shot of the game and it was enough to knock us out, in front of our own fans at Wembley. I could have done better for their goal and it was one of those mistakes I learned from and improved from it."

"The build-up before the game was unbearable at times, and a lot of people were talking as if we just had to turn up to qualify. Brian Clough had called Jan Tomaszewski a clown before the game, which had served to add fuel to the situation. He was actually a fair goalkeeper and proved that on the night, even though he did receive an awful lot of good fortune."

"It was just one of those nights where however many chances you create you are just not going to get the right result. We murdered them on the night and should have won by five. But Poland were no mugs at the time, they finished third in the World Cup, and we made them look very ordinary at Wembley."[31]

Peter Shilton

31   The DailyTelegraph. (2013) England v Poland: We murdered them in 1973 but they went to the World Cup. [Online] Available from: http://www.telegraph.co.uk/sport/football/teams/england/10375969/England-v-Poland-We-murdered-them-in-1973-but-they-went-to-the-World-Cup.html [Accessed: 21 November 2014].

"We had the makings of another great side like the World Cup-winning one of 1966. I really fancied our chances of going a long, long way and maybe even lifting the trophy. All we needed to do to get to West Germany was beat Poland at home by any score. It was the most one-sided international I ever played in but their goalkeeper was unbelievable. Although he made some great stops, he enjoyed a lot of luck. Some saves he did not have a clue about. The ball just hit him."

"I scored a penalty in the second half to equalise. I managed to send the 'keeper the wrong way. One hundred thousand people at Wembley with the nation expecting and World Cup qualification on the line — that's what you call pressure."

"Then, at 1-1, I struck a volley from inside the box which looked headed for the top right-hand corner. I had this habit of turning away to celebrate before the ball was in the net when I knew it was going in. The box was crowded with red and white shirts but I saw the flight of the ball towards the corner of the net and started to turn away. Suddenly, this yellow arm appeared from nowhere to divert the ball. At that moment, I feared we were not going to win."

"We were all very upset afterwards. I was supposed to film an advert for NatWest the following day. I just could not do it. There was nothing wrong with the selection or tactics. We played brilliant football. It was just one of those nights. The saddest thing was that it cost Sir Alf his job. That was diabolical. There is not another country in the world that would have got rid of such a brilliant manager. That really upset the lads. We would go through walls for him."[32]

Allan Clarke

"To this day, I wish I had kicked the ball out of play instead of putting my foot on it and trying to keep it in. I was trying to keep the attacking pressure on and got dispossessed. Peter Shilton, of course, should have thrown his cap on the ball. He was a great 'keeper, a class 'keeper, but he dived over it."

"I never forgot my mistake and as you can imagine playing for Leeds, I was not allowed to forget it. I received a lot of stick from opposition fans for a long time."

"We should have won. I never played in such a one-sided match, before or since. We had been so confident of winning. Personally, it was my big chance. I had been to two World Cups and never played because of the great Bobby Moore. West Germany would be different but it did not work out. That upset me tremendously."

"It was also very, very sad that it led to Sir Alf getting the sack. He was a great manager and a great man. Although I loved England, I played as much for him as I did for my country."

"At the end I was inconsolable. I did not cry. It would take a lot to make me cry. Bobby was the first to put his arm round

---

32   *Daily Mail.* (2013) *Shilton, Hunter and Clarke share their memories of England's 1973 World Cup qualification heartbreak.* [Online] Available from: http://www.dailymail.co.uk/sport/football/article-2458091/England-v-Poland-1973-Peter-Shilton-Norman-Hunter-Allan-Clarkes-memories-heartbreak.html [Accessed: 6 November 2014].

me. He did not say anything. There are occasions when you do not need to say anything. It took a long, long time for me to get over it."[33]

Norman Hunter

"Forty years on, people in Poland still call me the 'Hero of Wembley'."

"I'm proud my goal is still shown on TV as a symbol of us qualifying for the World Cup and knocking out England."

"I know everyone in England talks of Tomaszewski as the hero, but that's not fair on the rest of the team. It wasn't all down to one or two players – we achieved something special as a team."

"It is true Tomaszewski saved everything England could throw at him while, at the other end, I had one chance and I took it."

"But I did not like Brian Clough's comment about our goal-keeper being a clown. That was not correct, it was disrespect-ful. In sport, you should never describe your opponent in those terms when he is representing his country."

"But in any case, the 'clown' had the last laugh, didn't he?"

Jan Domarski

33   *Daily Mail.* (2013) *Shilton, Hunter and Clarke share their memories of England's 1973 World Cup qualification heartbreak.* [Online] Available from: http://www.dailymail.co.uk/sport/football/article-2458091/England-v-Poland-1973-Peter-Shilton-Norman-Hunter-Allan-Clarkes-memories-heartbreak.html [Accessed: 6 November 2014].

Too easily forgotten, after his lame effort to smother Domarski's shot, is that Shilton performed heroically, at the age of 40, against Poland to book Robson's side safe passage to Italy for the 1990 World Cup.

Domarski, however, will always be able to dine out on his most famous mistake. "Should Shilton have saved my shot? No – otherwise history might have been very different. If he had blocked it or parried it, we might not be talking about the game all these years later."[34]

34   *Daily Mirror.* (2013) *Poland's other 1973 hero Jan Domarski back to give England the spooks.* [Online] Available from: http://www.mirror.co.uk/sport/ football/england-v-poland-polands-1973-2368049 [Accessed: 29 July 2014].

"Like many football fans in this country (of a certain age), I can remember the 1973 game with a painful vividness. I was 10 years old and had returned to London, after three years abroad, in 1970 convinced that England was still one of the world's leading football nations. We had won the World Cup in 1966 and had been eliminated in 1970 by West Germany – but only after chucking away a two-goal lead, and because of the heat, and because our 'keeper had been poisoned by Mexican food. At Wembley, in the reassuring cold, against the Poles, there would be no mistake. The match, as I recall, was a siege of the Polish goal. England made chance after chance but could not score. Then two English errors and Poland broke away – and scored. We could only equalise but we needed the win. We were out.

At the time, it seemed like a heartbreaking aberration – a fluke that would never be repeated. But, with the benefit of hindsight, I can see that it was the beginning of a pattern that would become all too familiar over the next 40 years. England failed to qualify for the 1978 World Cup as well, and we also missed out in 1994. In between, there have been some good England sides – and some exciting matches – but the England team has never got further than the semi-finals of the World Cup."[35]

35   England, Poland, Nostalgia and National Destiny. October 2013. http://search.ft.com/search?q=v&t=all&fa=people%2Corganisations%2Cregions%2C-sections%2Ctopics%2Ccategory%2Cbrand&s=%2B*&f=brand%5B%22The+World%22%5D%5B%22The+World%22%5D&curations=ARTICLES%2C-BLOGS%2CVIDEOS%2CPODCASTS&highlight=true [accessed June 2014].

7.

WHERE WAS SIR ROBERT WHEN
HE WAS NEEDED?

Just seven years previously Bobby Moore had lifted the Jules Rimet Trophy high into the blue skies in July 66. It was England's greatest moment in their history and they were led by a young charismatic captain who was a natural leader of men. The name of Bobby Moore had had iconic status down the decades since that moment. When he died, his authority was maybe summed up by Jeff Powell who wrote after his early death from Prostate cancer in 1993 "Heaven's XI can now play. The captain has arrived".

In October 1973, he was now walking onto the pitch to console the players. Moore was still to play one more match in England colours (In November 73 v Italy at Wembley) but Moore's and England's decline was almost one and the same.

Moore was the Golden Boy of English football who grew into one of the world's greatest players by 1970 – a man of genuine global stature. In the match against Brazil in the World Cup of 1970, Moore's brilliance at reading a game was shown as Jairzinho raced at him with aggression and speed. Moore just stayed calm and timed his tackle to perfection. The man was "cool" under pressure and a man's man. At the end of the game, the World's great player, Pele, walked over to Moore and they swapped shirts and showed their mutual respect to the world. Here stood the world's greatest attacker and defender and they had just done battle.

By 1972, the signs were clearly evident of a decline in his game. He was still a fine leader but his game was not as sure and certain as in times gone by. In the game against West Germany in the European Championship he was caught overplaying in his own box and Germany punished the error. Two years earlier, he would have escaped with the ball and led England on a counter attack. In June 1973, Moore was caught again in possession; this time by a Polish attacker and he was left embarrassed as Poland scored their first goal in their important 2–0 win which also saw Alan Ball sent off.

By 1975, the great captain was no longer even playing in the First Division but in the Second Division with Fulham. He played against his beloved West Ham in the 1975 FA Cup Final. His decline was strange to watch. The legend that was Bobby Moore was playing in a league below his status and over the years to follow, the whole game in England shunned him. Maybe the best description appeared in the book *Harry* by Harry Rednapp (2013). Harry Rednapp played with Bobby Moore at West Ham and they remained friends. In his book, Rednapp writes with a care and admiration for his friend and Captain:

"What a man. I mean it. The straightest, most honest bloke you could meet in your life. Not an ounce of aggression in him, not a hint of nastiness. Won the World Cup, and even the opposition loved him. Brazilians idolised him. Not just Pele but all of them: Jairzinho, Rivelino. People say the 1970 Brazil team was the greatest of all time and Bob would have walked into it; in fact, he would have made the team of the tournament at any World Cup throughout history. I remember the game England played against Brazil that summer in Mexico. He was the best player on the field ... Everyone wanted to meet Bobby; everyone wanted a night out with him. And Bobby loved the social side of the game. He captained the England football team but he would have captained the England drinking team too if we had one ... You'd have thought that someone, somewhere, would have snapped Bobby up (after his retirement from playing) and given him a second chance. They only had to see him play to know the way he read and understood the game. And he was Sir Alf Ramsey's captain. That should have meant something. Surely? I won't have it that Bob couldn't have become a good manager. His footballing brain was on a different level when he played, so surely that would have converted to management, over time. To this day I will never know why he could not get a break. I still believe that with the right support, he could have been the greatest manager in West Ham's history. But we'll never know ... He could have been fantastic for England and for English football. Germany put Franz Beckenbauer centre stage. France did the same with Michel Platini, so much so that he ended up President of UEFA. Meanwhile, Bobby Moore holds the same rank of honour in this country as Des Lynam. How didn't he get a knighthood? Why didn't he get a knighthood? How did we end up with Sir Dave Richards and Sir Bert Millichip but not Sir Bobby Moore?

"We think of scandals in football as a player diving, or high transfer fees, but this, for me, is what scandal really means. The way that football treated Bobby, changed my attitude, professionally, because seeing him struggle confirmed to me that nobody in this game really gives a monkey's about you once you've served your purpose."[36]

It will always be hard to explain why the game in England did not nurture or even look after Bobby Moore better than they did. Many, including Rednapp, believe it was because of Moore's reputation for drinking. Maybe but there were many that liked to drink in all walks of life, including no few of England's leading politicians at the time – George Brown, Harold Wilson and Roy Jenkins to name a few. If this was really the reason, the level of hypocrisy in England would have been remarkable.

---

36   Redknapp, H. (ed.) (2013) *Always Managing: My Autobiography.* London: Edbury Press.

Maybe the problem was simpler? Moore simply stood taller than most. He was a natural leader and maybe most people would have been intimidated by his presence. Bobby Moore was a hero and sometimes it is hard for anyone to work with such characters as it presents a no win situation – if he does well, it is because he is a natural. If not, and many great players are not good managers, would you want to be the person to shoot the great legend? It was easier to look at other options.

This still does not excuse the fact that he was not recognised better and he could have been a superb coach and mentor. Moore's greatest talent lay in the fact that he could be one of the boys and yet lead them into battle with full respect the next day. Bobby Moore was a special leader because respect came from the man himself. It was not just that he was an exceptional player, but he would lead through example; he would rarely talk about his own problems but he would be there for his teammates and friends to support them; and he would not be fazed or intimidated in even the most pressurised of situations. In the previous chapter, it was noted how the tension and inexperience in the England team lead to their downfall. Bobby Moore was just 25 years old when he lifted the World Cup and he had played for England in the previous World Cup in 62.

Here is the debate – should Bobby Moore have captained England on 17 October 1973?

If the argument holds true that England's greatest weakness on that fateful night, then Moore's leadership could have made the difference, calmed the nerves and given strength to the team. Yes, Moore had been directly to blame for the first goal in the match against Poland in the June. Yes, he was also at fault against West Germany in the 72 Quarter Final at Wembley. Yes his game was in decline. But he was still good enough to be in the England squad and sat on the bench for the match at Wembley v Poland. And Poland had little intention of attacking England with the aggression they had shown in the intimidating environment that had existed in Katowice, when they played to the limits of the rules. Poland were a good team that defended that night in October. McFarland and Hunter were rarely troubled bar the one missed tackle. The England team played well, but missed one ingredient that Moore could bring – confidence under pressure, calmness and belief. Yes, Ramsey had stayed loyal – too loyal to his core team for too long – but maybe this was a one off match, unique in every way that needed the captain to be present. Peters was still in his infancy as an international captain and what was clearly missing was a man that could bring the individuals together as a unit. It can be soundly argued that England's greatest weakness over the whole of the 1970s was that the league was so competitive that it was tribal and that players struggled to come together as a united team at international level without leaders that stood beyond the petty competitiveness of the tribes.

Jeff Powell, in the *Daily Mail* (Nov 2012), noted how even the Scots respected Moore like few other Englishmen:

"The Scots never took to Alf but Bobby was a different matter. No matter how feisty the sporting enmity, admiration of greatness at the 'fitba' resides deep in their soul."

"The score that day was 5-0. Take good note of the nil."

"When, after games like this in which their finest foundered on his haughty defending and they called him 'that bastard Moore', it was said with enormous respect. When the bloody

English failed to knight him, the Scots were first to take to calling him 'Sir Robert.'"[37]

Moore had the aura about him that commanded respect. When he led a team, he looked confident, assured and as though he could face any opposition and still not be fazed. This presence could pull the team come together and with Peters, they could have provided the missing bedrock of experience to let the team attack with greater conviction and belief. Moore's qualities were needed for that one match.

Ramsey was a shrewd operator and manager. There would have been good reason why he stayed loyal to Bobby Moore for so long. He knew what Moore as captain brought to the team. The question is why he did not play Moore on that night? Did he believe that England were strong enough? Or maybe he underrated how nerves would affect his players or how the team would not come together?

It is likely that he had grown frustrated by Moore's increasing fallibility and the Poland match in the June and Moore's mistake had made Ramsey decide it was time to turn to Hunter. However, he seemed to underrate that the fact that Moore's very presence had been the glue that brought rival tribal players together as a unit. This may sound "over the top" but, as Ramsey and Revie would find, England's players struggled to play together with as much cohesion as they were used to playing with between 1965 and 1972. Under Revie, England rarely played as team. So what changed between 72 and the team that Greenwood built for 1982? Arguably, the missing calm presence of a captain such as Moore.

---

37   *Daily Mail.* (2012) *Jeff Powell: Sat alongside 99 schoolkids, Bobby Moore's dignified celebration of his 100 caps.* [Online] Available from: http://www.dailymail.co.uk/sport/football/article-2215262/Bobby-Moore-reached-100-caps-dignified-way-sharp-contrast-Ashley-Cole.html [Accessed: 7 November 2014].

Jeff Powell, Moore's biographer and friend, wrote in the *Daily Mail*:[38]

"Moore bought the guy a beer and said: 'You know, if you're quite good at something you don't have to tell everybody.'"

"Quite good? Of all the players in English football history, Moore is one of the elite who might have been forgiven for considering themselves worthy of just a modicum of special treatment. Not him."

"When he set the then record of 107 caps in a friendly against Italy in Turin in the June of 73, it was the press, again, who had to salute the achievement."

"We took a collection, bought an ornate piece of Capo de Monte porcelain and presented it to him back at the hotel after the match."

"The celebration went on until we boarded the buses to the airport the following morning – but the party was almost over."

"Moore had made a rare error – so rare as to be a collector's item – in a World Cup qualifier in Poland which preceded the Italy game. Ramsey dropped Moore for the return match at Wembley, only for his replacement Norman Hunter to make the identical mistake."

---

38   *Daily Mail.* (2012) *Jeff Powell: Sat alongside 99 schoolkids, Bobby Moore's dignified celebration of his 100 caps.* [Online] Available from: http://www.dailymail.co.uk/sport/football/article-2215262/Bobby-Moore-reached-100-caps-dignified-way-sharp-contrast-Ashley-Cole.html [Accessed: 7 November 2014].

"Thus England drew a match, in which Poland barely got out of their own half, and failed to qualify for the 1974 World Cup."

"There was one Wembley game left in 73, peculiarly another friendly with Italy. Ramsey recalled Moore as captain for what was to be his 108th and last cap — a world record at the time."

"'I sort of sensed it was the end,' said Bobby. 'But nothing was said on the night. I just went home.'"

"No grand farewell for a magnificent symbol of the national game. Not trumpets blaring. Just went home to wait for the letter."

"Back then, even the greatest players only found out whether they had been selected for the next England game when the envelope from the FA dropped through the letter box."

"For the first time since he made his England debut in the 1962 World Cup in Chile, the letter did not come. And that was the end of that."

"Imagine the indignant, affronted, self-righteous fury of Crass-ley (Ashley Cole) and JT – and Becks for that matter – if their England careers were abruptly ended without a personal, sympathetic conversation with the manager and a sycophantic tribute from the FA."

"Scotland's 'Sir' Bobby Moore simply said: 'The next World
Cup is four years away. It's time for younger guys, fresh faces.
I know they don't need old Mooro any more.'"

One wonders, as Ramsey reflected, what he would have changed for
the match. Maybe he just accepted defeat, but Moore and Ramsey
were connected. Both were perfect for each other. Both were graceful
– the acceptable face of England at its best. Both stood tall in their
moments of triumph and defeat. They were England's finest.

The match against Italy in the November proved to Moore's last
match but maybe the last hurrah should have been against Poland
and one suspects England would have won. He could then have
passed the baton over to Peters to lead the team into Germany 74.

""It is hard to look back. I remember meeting Martin Peters. The man just left me dazed with his presence. Then Bobby Moore joined him and I thought I was in the presence of gods. These guys made me and England proud. How do we repay them for giving us something so great? I won't hear a word against them. To me they were England and when they played I believed we could win against anyone. Fast-forward seven years and I was at Wembley as England were made to look like a Third Division team against the Dutch. How had we fallen so low so fast?"[39]

Charlie (Supporter)

8.

TIME FOR CHANGE

It was inevitable that Sir Alf Ramsey would not be given the time to rebuild the England side. In fairness, he had taken England to the summit and had overseen England play some of the finest football in its history. However, the last two years had seen a large decline in its standing in the world game and someone had to be accountable. After all, England had failed to qualify for the World Cup for the first time in its history and many felt shocked and bewildered. Change was inevitable, however much one admired Ramsey as a man and for his achievements.

Leo McKinstry – the author of *Sir Alf: A Major Reappraisal of the Life and Times of England's Greatest Football Manager*[40] – wrote an article in *The Guardian* in 2009:

"The 70s were a dark decade for English football, beset by problems such as hooliganism, dirty play, lack of cash and woeful performances by the national side. But one of the most powerful malignancies lurked within the Football Association itself, in the person of Professor Sir Harold Thompson, an Oxford chemistry don who had taught Margaret Thatcher when she was a student. Sir Harold was a bullying autocrat: 'He was a bastard. He treated the staff like shit,' said one former FA official."

40   The Guardian. (2009) *Hero cast aside – Sir Alf Ramsey, 1970s* [Online] Available from: http://www.theguardian.com/football/2009/may/21/seven-deadly-sins-football-alf-ramsey-england [Accessed: 21 November 2014].

"As FA chairman from 1976, Thompson ensured that Brian Clough never became England manager, even though Clough was by far the best candidate for the job. And in his role as a senior FA director before this, Thompson was also the driving force behind the sacking of Sir Alf Ramsey in 1974. Given England's failure to qualify for the World Cup that year, Ramsey's dismissal may have been justified, but the whole episode was handled with brutal insensitivity. Despite having won the World Cup for England in 1966, Ramsey was kicked out after 11 years of unstinting service and unprecedented success with a pay out of £8,000 and a meagre annual pension of £1,200. In his last year as England boss, his salary was a pitiful £7,200 – less than some Division Three managers were earning. To add insult to injury, Don Revie, Alf's permanent successor, was paid £25,000."

"The FA's shabby behaviour was largely down to Thompson, who had developed an intense animosity towards Ramsey. Part of this was due to nothing more than snobbery. Though Sir Alf spoke in the clipped manner of an army officer, he was from a deprived Dagenham background. But Thompson was obsessed with public school and university pedigree. 'He always referred to me, even to my face, as Ramsey, which I found insulting,'[41] Sir Alf once said. An incident during an Eastern Europe tour in 1972 crystallised the hostility between the two men. At breakfast in the team's hotel one morning, Thompson was smoking a large cigar. The players found the smoke unpleasant and, on their behalf, Ramsey asked him

---

41   The Guardian. (2009) *Hero cast aside – Sir Alf Ramsey, 1970s* [Online] Available from: http://www.theguardian.com/football/2009/may/21/seven-deadly-sins-football-alf-ramsey-england [Accessed: 21 November 2014].

to put it out. Thompson did so but was infuriated to have been shown such disrespect. Sir Alf's fate was sealed from that moment. Soon Thompson was waging an internal campaign to have the England manager ousted. The exit from the World Cup allowed him to force the hand of his fellow FA directors and Sir Alf's sacking was agreed in April 1974."

"After brief management spells with Birmingham City and Greek club Panathinaikos, Ramsey slipped into semi-retirement, living in his modest Ipswich home and struggling on his small pension before succumbing to Alzheimer's. England's greatest ever manager deserved so much better. He was a true hero, but thanks to Thompson, he became an outcast. The late Alan Ball, one of Ramsey's World Cup winners, said the treatment of Sir Alf was 'the most incredible thing that ever happened in English football.'"

One of the strangest and hardest factors to explain in this story is how some of England's true heroes were not just side-lined but treated so very badly. Sir Alf, Bobby Moore and Martin Peters. All their top-level careers were effectively over by 1975. Peters joined Norwich, Moore was with Fulham and Sir Alf was as good as put out to pasture. Whatever the rights and wrongs of what took place and what would go on to take place over the next forty years, the teams 1966 and 1970 stand tall almost without comparison in England's history. The only teams that may challenge them was Robson's 1990 team and Venables team of 1996, which showed potential but never had the chance to realise it. The vast majority would support the 1970 team over the 1990 team for skill, and ability. The 1996 team would be a step behind both.

And here lies the heart of the story. The players may have not been ready, experienced enough or even good enough for the 1973 match; Ramsey may have made a mistake in not playing Moore, but the thing that let England down the most was the structure and arrogance that lay within the management of the game itself in this country. England's failure was not expected or foreseen. The preparation for internationals was simply not good enough. Ramsey had to work within the tightest of preparation times – but most importantly, the English game believed its own hype. The structure of the game did not help support and develop players from being excellent club players into becoming international players. International football was a very different prospect to club football and other European countries were developing programmes that focused on players to a higher degree than in England. In England, the philosophy was one of "sink or swim". Too many talented players have England careers that only hint of what could have been possible. Martin Chivers and Allan Clarke could have been a world-class strike force but needed more experience and time. History has shown that it takes time – and often failure – for great players to emerge. Too often the players not allowed either.

Over the years and in the decade, English club teams enjoyed great success and it was asked time and again why did club success on the European stage not translate to the international team? The answer is very simple – the structure was complacent, even arrogant and did not give enough support and preparation for the international team.

It can be easily seen today when one sees the structure that the modern FA provide; how both the England Cricket players possess central contracts to the ECB and how the RFU really have invested in player development. They make the 1970s FA look like an organization out of the dark ages – ignorant and amateurish in approach – and the truth is that they were. Just consider:

- Why did some of England's greatest players not play for the leading clubs? Banks with Stoke City: Hurst with West Ham: Peters with West Ham and Spurs; Moore with West Ham. These were world-class players and they played with teams that would rarely compete at the top of the game. Why did the top clubs not want these players?
- Why was Peters' international career over at the age of just 30? This was a man seen as "ten years ahead of his time" and would still play exceptional football for Norwich City in later years.
- Why was Geoff Hurst the only one of the great players to become associated with the England team (Hurst became a coach to England under Greenwood)? Why weren't the talents and knowledge of Banks, Moore and Peters better maintained? They had so much to give and it was wasted.
- Banks, Moore, Peters and Ball were just as important to England's success as Bobby Charlton and Geoff Hurst. Why were Hurst and Charlton knighted and others not? Where is the consistency or fairness in approach? Does this say that scoring three goals on one day is better and more important that captaining your country – as Moore and Peters did – and play roles that led to those goals. Peters also scored in the Final.
- How has football nurtured the retired great players of that era so that could add value to future generations?
- What was the legacy of the 1966 triumph?
- What did Ramsey do which was so bad that he left almost forgotten after his exit as manager?

The Hard truth is English football failed England in 1973.

"It was the most devastating half-hour of my life," Ramsey later said of his sacking. "I stood in a room almost full of staring committee men. It was just like I was on trial. I thought I was going to be hanged."[42]

How sad and ridiculous. Allan Clarke would later comment:

"But the way the FA sacked Sir Alf a few months later saddened me. Only in England would we treat a World Cup winner like that."[43]

Ramsey would have been happy that his players saw and recognised his value. In some ways, Ramsey was a contradiction. He was a boy from Dagenham who played his football for Southampton, Tottenham Hotspur and England. As a manager he guided the unglamorous Ipswich Town from the Third Divison to become Champions of England. Logic would say here was a hard working, tough working class man who had achieved success and yet he spoke like an English Public School boy. He had taken lessons to learn how to speak well, but this in turn suggests a dedicated, pragmatist who understood what was required to be successful.

It could also indicate a man that wished to socially climb, except Ramsey rarely pushed himself forward and was quietly spo-

---

42   *The Guardian.* April 1999. *Lancaster Gate plottings that ended the reign of England's most successful manager.* http://www.theguardian.com/football/1999/apr/25/newsstory.sport9 [accessed: September 2014].

43   *Daily Mirror.* (2012) *Sir Alf axe STILL hurts: Allan Clarke on the loss that lead to World Cup hero's sacking* [Online] Available from: http://www.mirror.co.uk/sport/football/news/england-football-team-allan-clarke-1380243 [Accessed: 1 November 2014].

ken. Ramsey understood that one had to change and adapt to be successful.

There is a story of a journalist who saw Sir Alf on the platform waiting for the train from London to Ipswich. They said hello and shared a drink together on the train to Ipswich. As the journalist recounted the story, Ramsey was calm and polite throughout and openly discussed football. As they reached Ipswich, Sir Alf bade farewell and went on this way. A few hours later, the journalist had learnt that Ramsey had been sacked just prior to their encounter and yet he showed no self-pity, and just spoke of others. It is similar to the moment after the final whistle of the Poland match when Ramsey calmly walked over to shake the hand of the Polish coach. This was a man that accepted both triumph and defeat with equal measure. This was a man that understood success and failure.

Trevor Brooking, the former England player and pundit once said about Sir Alf:[44]

"Sir Alf was heavily criticised for failing to qualify for West Germany 74 – but Poland proved in the finals, when they went on to the latter stages, that they were a world-class side."

"Even if you took away the 1966 success you would have to say that Sir Alf was one of the very best England managers – because in 1970 he achieved one of our best performances in an overseas World Cup."

"Perhaps his greatest skill was his man-management. It's odd, because he wasn't like your typical manager. He was a very

44   BBC Archive http://news.bbc.co.uk/1/hi/sport/football/332811.stm [accessed September 2014].

quietly spoken man, but he had this presence, an emphatic manner, that you just couldn't ignore."

"He also had a tremendous sense of loyalty. Throughout his time with England he was criticised for staying with certain players – but by doing that he created a strong bond with them."

"Despite fluctuations in club form he stuck with the players he knew and that bred a superb spirit, which was one of the secrets of the team's success."

"I made my England debut under Sir Alf. It was against Portugal in April 1974, a matter of weeks before he was sacked. We'd already been knocked out of the World Cup and he used the opportunity to bring in a number of younger players. His great skill was to make you feel as if he'd been focusing on you for a while. Straight away he told you what he thought your strengths were and made it clear that you were a valued member of the squad."

"There was a real element of trust involved. He made you think that he wasn't a manager who believed in chopping and changing, so you felt you were there to stay."

"There is a sense that English football did not treat Sir Alf as well as it could have done after he left the national job. As with my former West Ham boss Ron Greenwood, I think he should have been given a national coaching role. But the problem for Sir Alf was he didn't have a great relationship with the football establishment. Some people within the FA didn't feel close to him, so as soon as there was the first hiccup in results there was a parting of ways. But that was the thing – he was a players' man, not an Establishment man."

On 1 May, Joe Mercer was appointed as the interim England manager. It was a tough assignment to take over from a great manager in Sir Alf that the players loved and morale would have been low. But Mercer was a good appointment – a former international player who made five appearances for England between 1938–39 and 27 wartime appearances. He had been a successful club manager who enjoyed great success with Manchester City between 1965–71 where he won the League Title in 1968, the FA Cup in 1969, the European Cup Winners Cup in 1970 and the League Cup in 1970.

Mercer's England played some great football and began to play with vigour and confidence once again. In his seven matches in charge, England won three, Drew three and lost one. The FA was relieved to see a brighter picture emerge and the reviews from journalists were very impressive. Mercer came from the Ramsey school in that he understood players. He was, however, different to Ramsey in that he was less aloof. He was a more highly-strung man with nervous energy but the players could see he lived and breathed the game. Players liked playing for him. He also had the advantage that he was not a club manager and therefore the traditional intense rivalries between clubs had no real effect on Mercer. He stood above it and the players needed to know that the England set up was very separate to the club environment.

Mercer was open to taking the role on a permanent basis but the FA had courted Don Revie who accepted the position.

The Guardian ran a descriptive article about Mercer's short

36-day reign as England manager under the title. The article tells the story with feeling and depth: The Forgotten story ... England under Joe Mercer.[45]

> "In December 1981 *The Observer* ran Hugh McIlvanney's elegy for Muhammad Ali after the great fighter's career-ending defeat by Trevor Berbick in the Bahamas under the headline 'The king who went out on a dustcart'. Most recent accounts of the sacking of Sir Alf Ramsey as England's manager on 1 May 1974 adopt the same tone, summoning a mixture of regret and indignation at such shabby maltreatment."

> "When reading the statement put out by the Football Association's international committee, under the imperious influence of Sir Harold Thompson, to announce the 1966 World Cup winner's dismissal, one concedes the validity of their disgust."

> "'Committees of the FA, which have been considering the future of English football,' it read in Kremlin-apparatchik charmless prose, 'have examined some aspects in detail and progress has been made. At a meeting on 14 February the executive committee set up a sub-committee with the following terms of reference: To consider our future policy in respect of the promotion of international football. Following meetings, a unanimous recommendation was submitted to the executive committee that Sir Alf Ramsey should be replaced as the England team manager. The recommendation

---

45   *The Guardian.* (2012) *The forgotten story of ... England under Joe Mercer.* [Online] Available from: http://www.theguardian.com/sport/blog/2012/oct/11/forgotten-story-joe-mercer-england-manager [Accessed: 30 October 2014].

was accepted unanimously by the executive committee.' Colin Crompton could not have put it more mellifluously."

"And yet this sense of disservice is revisionist. Since April 1972, when Günter Netzer had orchestrated West Germany's 3–1 evisceration of England at Wembley in the first leg of the European Championship quarter-final, it had become quite common to read that Ramsey had outlived his usefulness. The away leg, a 0–0 draw for which the manager had picked Arsenal's Peter Storey and Leeds United's Norman Hunter in midfield, was littered with so many England fouls that the correspondent of the biggest selling newspaper of the day, Alan Hoby of the Sunday Express, wrote: 'I felt embarrassed and ashamed by the Englishmen's violent, ugly methods.'"

"After the draw with Poland in 1973, Ramsey lingered for six months while England's absence for the first time from a World Cup Finals tournament that they had deigned to enter sank in. The Poland game provoked a withering editorial from Foul magazine. 'Dirty defensive play was actually programmed into the English tactical plan before the match began … so when we say that Alf must go, it's not purely because we want to see England's football lifted out of the sterile unimaginative rut … it's not because English supporters would like to see wing-halves and flank forwards given a chance to establish themselves before they become extinct … it is because the whole idea of using illegal tactics as a defensive ploy to cover for the inadequacies at the back, and to incapacitate the opposition from keeping our forwards out, is sickening and a travesty of the way football should be played.'"

"The motive, then, was perceived as just even if the FA's method was typically ignominious. Ramsey's employers kept him hanging on for two more matches after the conclusion of the World Cup qualifying group, a 1–0 defeat at home by Italy to close 1973 in which Bobby Moore won his last cap and a 0–0 draw with Portugal in Lisbon the following spring when the manager, perhaps keen to indicate conspicuously that he was demonstrably not yesterday's man, sloughed off his hidebound reputation and gave debuts to Phil Parkes, Mike Pejic, Martin Dobson, Dave Watson, Stan Bowles and Trevor Brooking. His attempt at rejuvenation, however, was in vain. The FA had come to its decision even before England took the field at the Estádio da Luz."

"Thompson had, according to Brian Glanville and Leo McKinstry, borne a grudge ever since Ramsey had asked the FA chairman to extinguish the cigar he was smoking at the breakfast table in the team hotel after the players had complained about the fumes. 'Sir Alf's fate was sealed from that moment,' wrote McKinstry. Thompson, the vice-president of St John's College, Oxford, had been enraged by Ramsey's lack of deference."

"There is something hilariously hypocritical about Thompson's concept of respect and his behaviour towards England's managers. Ramsey – who was knighted in 1967, a year before Thompson – was insulted by the committeeman's insistence on always referring to him by surname alone. At an official dinner in 1976 when Don and Elsie Revie were sitting next to Thompson, Ramsey's eventual long-term successor objected to his employer's supercilious schoolmasterly form of address. 'When I get to know you better, Revie, I shall call you Don,' Thompson pompously said. In a brilliant but reckless reply, Revie said: 'When I get to know you better, Thompson, I will call you Sir Harold.'"

"Analysing Ramsey's sacking and the part prickly relations between the two knights played in it, Glanville wrote: 'Thompson was surely right, but probably right for the wrong reasons.' The FA settled Ramsey's £7,200-a-year contract, paying the 54-year-old a lump sum of £8,000 and granted him an annual pension of £1,200. By comparison, when Revie was appointed he told the FA the salary might just pass muster in Division Three but First Division managers were on considerably higher wages. After negotiation, Revie and the FA settled on £25,000 a year, slightly higher than the top-flight average but much less than the £50,000 signing-on fee plus £31,500-a-year deal Everton had offered Revie in the summer of 1973. That 240 percent increase on the England manager's salary was symptomatic of a governing body that had exploited Ramsey's sense of duty and it was how the FA treated him as a man rather than as a manager that drew most censure."

"For years at formal briefings Ramsey had treated criticism with contempt and adopted a brooding aloofness that conveyed his impatience and scorn. Informally he could, said David Lacey, 'be an engaging conversationalist if caught in the right mood and at the right moment'. The public, though, who were dependent on the filter of the media and the bear-baiting derision of ITV pundits such as Malcolm Allison and Brian Clough, could be forgiven for wanting a respite from Ramsey's defensiveness and taciturnity. The leading candidates to replace him – Leicester's Jimmy Bloomfield, Coventry's Gordon Milne, Gordon Jago of QPR, Burnley's Jimmy Adamson and Bolton's Jimmy Armfield – all offered the opportunity of a generational shift and most of them an affability alien to Ramsey. It was too late, though, to conclude negotiations with any of them or their clubs before the Home Championship and the summer tour, so the FA resolved to appoint a caretaker and chose the epitome of cordiality and benevolence, luring Joe Mercer out of semi-retirement as the general manager of Coventry City to hold the fort."

"The contrast with Ramsey was marked at his first press conference. 'His humour has fluttered happily about the stage recently vacated by the serious monologist,' wrote *The Observer's* Peter Corrigan. 'Kind words and patted backs have added gaiety to the atmosphere and we are near the realisation of the worst fears of those who equate his temporary appointment as England team manager to Uncle Remus doing holiday relief for Genghis Khan.'"

"At the age of 59 when he agreed to take the post, Mercer had spent the past 43 years in football, first as an attacking wing-half with the Everton side who won the title in 1938–39 before losing the cream of his career to military service during the Second World War, then winning two more league championships as Arsenal's captain in 1947–48 and 1952–53. After a year spent running his grocery business on retirement, he was appointed manager of Sheffield United, moving to Aston Villa following three and a half seasons at Bramall Lane."

"At Villa Park he built a competitive and talented young side who were dubbed, given the fad for alliterative nicknames such as Drake's Ducklings and the Busby Babes, the Mercer Minors. He won the first League Cup with Villa in 1961 but was sacked in July 1964 after returning from a sabbatical he had been forced to take to recover from a nervous breakdown. Although he was advised by his doctor to forgo completely the stresses of management he applied for and was appointed Manchester City's manager in 1965 where, in tandem with Allison, the visionary coach he hired as soon as he got the job, he almost went through the card in trophies – Second Division title, Football League Championship, FA, League and Cup Winners' Cups."

"His contribution to City was commemorated in the Kippax tribute still sung at the Etihad to the tune of Auld Lang Syne: 'The Stretford End cried out aloud: "It's the end of you Sky Blues." Joe Mercer came. We played the game. We went to Rotherham, we won 1–0 and we were back into Division One. We've won the League, we've won the Cup, we've been to Europe too. And when we win the League again we'll sing this song to you: City, City, City." Note the lack of any mention for Allison there. By 1970 the coach was exasperated at the perception that his influence was inferior to Mercer's and agitated to succeed his boss. After a couple of years of politicking, with the two men aligned to battling boardroom factions, Allison got his way and Mercer was stripped of responsibility for the first team in October 1971. 'I still believe I have a lot to offer', he said. 'I'm a tactician not an administrator and don't really see myself as a general manager.' But a general manager he became, seeing out the season in which City's title bid stalled after the signing of Rodney Marsh, before leaving for Coventry to mentor Milne."

"Anyone who thought that, at his age and with his mobility restricted by chronic sciatica, Mercer would be happy to take his role literally by doubling up as the team's protector and maintenance man was quickly disabused. 'I have given a lot of thought to my task,' he said, 'and psychologically I have to make sure that the loyalty these players gave to Alf lives on for the next manager. Anything I add to the excellent organisation Alf left behind must be a natural extension of it. Tactics, after all, are there as a base from which players can express themselves naturally.'"

"The squad at his disposal had been picked by Ramsey 12 days before his sacking was announced. Mercer's demand that the 20-strong selection expressed themselves naturally and his instruction at their first gathering were the fundamentals of the philosophy he adopted for his 36 days in charge. 'Let's all at least bloody smile, eh lads?' he said to them."

"For his first match against Wales at Ninian Park, Mercer opted for a three-man forward line of Mick Channon, Stan Bowles and Kevin Keegan, the latter winning only his third cap in three years, oddly all against Wales. Leaving out Martin Peters and thus breaking the chain with 1966, Mercer had said that he would select players of quality and verve and was true to his word. Wales, who hadn't scored a goal for 364 days, were easily outplayed but, paradoxically for David Lacey given Mercer's emphasis on attack, the defence, and Colin Todd in particular, deserved most credit. Although Bowles opened the scoring in the first half, it gave a misleading gloss to an otherwise disjointed contribution from the QPR attacker. More significantly was the identity of the second scorer, Keegan with his first for England after sticking out a foot to meet David Nish's cross. 'Having sacked the producer and thrown away the script,' wrote Lacey in The Guardian, 'England could hardly have hoped for more than a series of impromptu sketches and if this was the sum of their ambitions they were not to be disappointed.'"

"Expected to experiment four days later against Northern Ireland at Wembley, Mercer picked the same team, again awarding Emlyn Hughes the captaincy, sticking with three of Derby County's back four and issuing Keegan with another licence to roam. But it was the player best known to Mercer, Manchester City's tireless midfield dynamo Colin Bell, who had the greatest impact by establishing dominance in midfield thanks to his tenacity for winning possession and his powerful, surging breaks upfield. Keegan, too, managed to reproduce some of his trademark club darts behind the full-backs but was too often let down by the service of a team that sent in too many crosses for one without an orthodox centre-forward, centres that Pat Jennings easily thwarted. Mercer resolved this after 55 minutes, 'at a stroke', he said, by replacing Bowles with Leicester City's Frank Worthington who was deadly in the air, a quality his misleading reputation as a flick-obsessed showman has obscured. Fourteen minutes into his debut Worthington rose beyond the far post to direct a header from Channon's cross towards his club-mate Keith Weller who nodded the ball past Jennings in a goal conceived at Filbert Street."

"Two games for Mercer and two victories with enough grounds for optimism to keep his smiling face in the papers appended to his anointment as 'Uncle Joe'. But the real test was still to come, England's five-match run as jilted warm-up man for teams who had qualified for the World Cup in West Germany. Scotland came first but before the caretaker faced his first traditional Hampden Park reception, he had to deal with Bowles, who had absconded from the team's Welwyn hotel two nights before the game to go to the dogs at White City. Asked by a reporter who spotted him whether he intended to return to fly to Scotland the next day, he said: 'No.' He later rang Mercer to apologise and issued a statement saying: 'I left the England party yesterday because I was sick and depressed. It has always been my ambition to play for England, particularly at Wembley, and no one can know how I felt when I was taken off.' Mercer accepted the apology, saying: 'It's sad isn't it?' then told Bowles there was no way back under his management."

Worthington started against Scotland in Bowles's place, with Peters in for Keegan and Norman Hunter for the injured Roy McFarland, but England failed comprehensively on a sodden pitch to match Scotland's flexibility, the pace of the rampaging full-backs Danny McGrain and Sandy Jardine and the central midfield control seized by Billy Bremner and Davie Hay. They were 2–0 down after 30 minutes and, though Dave Watson's introduction at half-time to replace Hunter and end the experiment with two number sixes at the heart of defence, stemmed the Scottish tide, the nearest England came to goals were rare headers from Peters and Worthington. Lacey, citing Harold Pinter's The Caretaker, highlighted the team's lack of fluency: 'England did not play badly in their makeshift mundane way; but in the hands of their caretaker they have become a team of Davises, each with an idea of how to get to Sidcup, none with the means, on his own, of putting the operation into practice.'

"Argentina's visit to Wembley on the Wednesday night following the defeat at Hampden Park was their first since the ill-tempered World Cup quarter-final in 1966 that is for ever linked with Antonio Rattín's sending-off and Ramsey's excoriation of England's opponents as 'animals'. So raw were Argentina's wounds that they agreed to stop off en route to West Germany only if an Argentinian refereed the game. This precondition proved crucial."

"With Nish injured, Hughes moved to right-back where he was partnered, on the opposite flank, by his Anfield team-mate Alec Lindsay. Keegan, Channon and Worthington were given the opportunity to impress up front, with the graceful Brooking, after a long campaign by Glanville, at last given the role of midfield creator to dovetail with Keegan's clever exploitation of space. England went ahead seconds before half-time, Bell rolling a pass behind Argentina's defence for Channon to race on to, round the 'keeper and score. As the players trooped off for half-time, Hughes pushed his counterpart, the captain Roberto Perfumo, in the midst of an argument, only for his other counterpart, the right-back Rubén Glaria, to end the row by smacking Hughes in the face. Remarkably the referee, Arturo Iturralde, chose to ignore this and Argentina defused the situation by replacing Glaria for the second half."

"England's slick passing and movement made another inroad 10 minutes after the break from a corner won when Worthington latched on to Brooking's excellent penetrative pass. Keegan took it short and when the ball was clipped into the penalty area it bounced up in front of Bell who smashed a shot against the underside of the crossbar and left Worthington to turn the ball in with an acrobatic flick of his left foot. Mario Kempes got one back four minutes later, steering home his shot from 15-yards after Peter Shilton had palmed out a cross to his feet. But with only a minute of the match remaining and England looking more confident and commanding than they had done for more than a year against such good opposition, Kempes struck again. "Having taken too much time to control René Houseman's cross, Kempes was tackled by Hughes, seemingly fairly. But such was the flourish with which the centre-forward threw himself to the turf, the referee, Kempes' countryman, was persuaded to award a penalty despite the England captain's impassioned protestations. The crowd clearly thought Kempes had dived, booing him as he ran up to take the penalty, continuing after he smacked it past Shilton and building to a climax moments later at the conclusion of the match. Yet despite conceding an undeserved draw, England's spirit, coherence and occasional flamboyance suggested the players were beginning to break the bonds of caution and rigidity."

"Mercer flew with the squad to Leipzig for the first leg of their tour, where they took on East Germany, who would defeat their neighbours, hosts and eventual winners, West Germany, in the group stage of the World Cup. After playing in all four of Mercer's games, Keith Weller's international career ended with him being dropped for Martin Dobson who won his second cap, this time in front of a crowd of 100,000 at Zentralstadion."

"With Worthington, Keegan and Channon again selected up front, as they would be for all three games in eastern Europe, England picked up where they had left off against Argentina, tearing the East Germany defence apart and beating a tattoo on the woodwork, hitting the bar and a post twice each. The movement of the front three caused havoc, creating opportunities for Dobson, Brooking and Bell to shoot as well as repeatedly carving out chances for themselves. And yet they fell behind in the second half to Joachim Streich's goal 24 minutes from time. It took 90 seconds for England to rally, Channon equalising direct from a free-kick with a scorching shot, and though a draw was disappointing given their excellence and ebullience, Mercer was heartened by the performance. 'We hit the woodwork more times than a team of lumberjacks,' he said ruefully. 'An old-fashioned manager and old-fashioned posts.'"

"In *The Observer* Corrigan noted that the caretaker had been treated to a bottle of champagne after the match to celebrate England's exhilarating display. 'The cork popped with such force it hit the ceiling and rebounded into the company. 'Christ, we've hit the post again,' Mercer said. With a spirit of adventure restored to the side, one shy FA official told Lacey: 'I haven't enjoyed a game so much for years.'"

"Keeping the same line-up for the match in Sofia against Bulgaria, England came away with a 1–0 victory that flattered their hosts. Again the interchanging of Keegan, Worthington and Channon flummoxed the opposition and, with Bell, Dobson and Brooking sharing an ability to find the front men, England destroyed the Bulgarian defenders' positional discipline. Worthington scored by beating the offside trap before calmly finishing when one-on-one with the 'keeper but it was Channon's marauding running and deft manipulation of the ball that enchanted the crowd."

"Apart from a problem over accommodation in Sofia, eventually sorted out when the squad was given the press's hotel and the journalists each given three bottles of beer to compensate for their relegation for a night into inferior digs, there had been no hitches on the tour. All that changed the morning after they had defeated Bulgaria when they arrived at Belgrade airport. Keegan, like the rest of the squad, was not wearing his England tie or blazer, a sartorial lapse with unpleasant consequences. While waiting for his luggage he sat down near the baggage carousel while a couple of his team-mates messed about on the conveyor belt. Keegan was promptly arrested by Yugoslavia's border police and taken to a back room, where he was punched, kicked and truncheoned before being charged with sexually assaulting a stewardess, a further assault on a guard, disturbing the peace and causing an obstruction. The players refused to abandon him to his fate and FA officials, British embassy staff and Mercer eventually persuaded Keegan's captors that he was innocent and should be released."

"Keegan, battered, bleeding and shaken, was not, however, spooked by his experience when he took to the field. Keeping an unchanged side for the third game in succession England once again impressed, this time as much for their fortitude as their new-found attacking adroitness. Channon put them 1–0 up from a corner before Yugoslavia had hit their stride, spurring the hosts to up the ante with some sublime, inventive passing and intelligent runs. They equalised before half-time and took the lead when Brane Oblak hit a thunderous 25-yard shot past Ray Clemence in the second half."

"England, less assured than they had been during the preceding three games, attempted to gain a foothold back in the match by using Channon's pace to try to stretch the opposition defence but they were too canny and too often ushered him down a cul-de-sac. Throwing on a substitute for the first time since Hampden, Mercer sent on Malcolm MacDonald for Worthington and after 10 minutes the replacement found Keegan, who scored England's second with a thumping diving header. At the death MacDonald bullocked through the offside trap only to spurn the chance to win the match by snatching at his shot and England ended the tour with a creditable draw."

"And that was the end of Mercer's mission. The FA was so impressed by the friendly atmosphere he had fostered that questions about the possibility of Mercer taking the job on a longer-term basis, with his Coventry protégé Gordon Milne as the straight man in the double act, were not immediately quashed. Mercer, too, seemed open to persuasion but the FA was working on another plan, putting out feelers to the most successful English club manager available, Leeds United's Revie, which ultimately proved fruitful even if Lancaster Gate subsequently had grave cause to regret its choice."

"Mercer went back to Highfield Road, thanked for putting the smile back on the face of English football during what Glanville vividly called his 'beguiling interregnum'. Moreover he had established a platform for more freewheeling talents in the side, a sadly short-lived achievement as far as Worthington was concerned but one, which benefited Keegan and Channon. Just as importantly – though it proved ephemeral – was giving England their dignity back on the eve of a World Cup at which they would be bystanders. It had been all very well for England to refuse invitations to the World Cup before the Second World War, but one must emphasise how deep the sense of humiliation felt was, by the realisation that they were too damn ugly to attend the global television party."

"'I didn't want this bloody job in the first place,' Mercer had told the players, naturally with a smile, at their first meeting. By succeeding at restoring their reputation, however briefly, the reluctant caretaker did more than keep the house in order. He gave them a blueprint for renovation that was disastrously ignored when the caution and anxiety he had temporarily banished returned with a vengeance."

Mercer had started rebuilding the England side very effectively. He had introduced new players that possessed flair, and the imagination to unlock well organised international teams and a confidence was beginning to flow in England's play – a confidence that had been missing for some time.

Life is easy in hindsight but maybe the FA should have persevered with Mercer. English football had become so tribal that it would take characters of stature to bring teams together effectively. Mercer had proven that he could achieve this. He was respected and liked by the players just as Ramsey was. His track record was there and he possessed a maturity that allowed him to be a father figure, who could heal the wounds from the sadness of the performances of 1972 and 1973. England needed time to lick their wounds and heal. Mercer was the father figure allowing this and it needed more time.

Although, at the time, of his appointment as interim manager he was general manager of Coventry City, he was seen to be above the fierce club rivalries of the time. It is no coincidence that Greenwood was able to rebuild England into a competitive team on the world stage. Greenwood had left the club stage and was in an administrative role with West Ham with John Lyall as manager. Due to the nature of the English league, the England manager had to be seen to be bigger and outside the influences of the club game and in turn such characters could unite individuals for England. Mercer was doing exactly this in his 36 days.

Of course there was logic in appointing Don Revie. Leeds were the outstanding club side of the era but Leeds did not win friends well. They were aggressive, intimidating, competitive and formidable. They possessed a win at all costs approach and Revie was the man that had built this spirit in the team. One of the most vivid examples of the emotions that this could conjure up would have been Brian Clough's brief 44 days as Leeds manager in succession to Revie. On the day Clough was sacked by Leeds, both men appeared on TV together and the clash was bitter. Of course, there was real background. Clough should have been a candidate for the England job. Clough mistrusted Revie and did not like his methods and he had just been sacked by Leeds after so short a time.

An article in *Sport Magazine* described the tension.[46]

> "This is the big daddy of all the rivalries. They loathed each other. The irony is that they came from very similar working-class backgrounds. They were both born in the same area of Middlesbrough, just a long goal-kick apart. You would think they might have things in common. But, of course, they were fantastically different personalities."

> "The loathing started with Clough, and there are various theories as to why. Ultimately, he didn't like the way Don Revie's Leeds team played football: the hard men who were niggly and physical and tried to con referees. That shaped his utter dislike of Revie. Clough had a very pure idea of how football

46   *Sport Magazine*. October 2013 http://issuu.com/sportmagazine/docs/ sport_magazine_325_ [accessed April 2014].

should be played: on the ground, that players should behave themselves on the pitch and so on. He thought Revie's tactics were a betrayal of football."

"Also, according to [Clough biographer] Duncan Hamilton, Clough once saw the referee talking to Revie before a match and reckoned that he was trying to turn the referee. Duncan thought all things sprung from that, and he knew Clough quite well. Now, it may have been that Clough was mistaken in what he saw – and I have to say that I could never pin down a particular incident of this. But I do know that, up until about 1968–69, Clough almost revered Revie – so something definitely changed."

TV Showdown

"Famously, on the day Clough was sacked from Leeds in 1974, Calendar, the local TV programme, managed to get the two of them to debate on air. If you watch it, you can sense the hostility between them. Particularly from Revie, actually. Because as Clough arrived at the studio that night, he'd been sacked and he was very disappointed – but also a bit relieved, and he'd had a few drinks. Revie, on the other hand – an England manager who was preparing for the next match against Czechoslovakia – was resentful. He felt that Clough had taken a club that he'd moulded into one of the best in Europe and ruined it in 44 days."

"Revie will have heard all the stories about how Clough had told all the players: 'You can chuck all your medals in the bin, because you won them by cheating.' He was dismayed. If, up to then, it had been Clough resentful of Revie, that interview showed that it was now about Revie's anger at Clough. It was the lowest ebb in their relationship. And, after that, they just avoided each other. They had different outlooks on life, different personalities. They wanted nothing to do with each other after that day in 1974."

(2013)

Of course, the view from many was that the England camp had become too cosy under Ramsey and need a shake up. But this did not change the fact that, just like Clough, many players had reservations about both Revie's and Leed's approach. It would not be easy to just place these feelings to one side.

Would Clough have been a better appointment than Revie?

It would have been a bold appointment and one that would have gone against the nature of the FA. The argument for Clough was that he had shown that he could build teams that played football in the right spirit and manner. He believed in technique and the passing game. He was also young and would have broken the mould of what Ramsey had built, which – if the FA were concerned was too cosy – would have shaken things up. But he was so outspoken he alienated many. His greatest days were still ahead of him with his leadership of Nottingham Forest and the way to took them from the Second Division to become European Cup Winners two years in a row (1979 and 1980). He was then at the peak of his powers and Peter Swales, the former Manchester City Chairman and a member of the FA committee that selected the England manager, admitted that he Clough gave the best interview when he was a candidate for the job in 1978. It is often said that Clough was the "greatest England manager that they never had," but in 1978, the FA made the right choice with Ron

Greenwood. Should Clough have got the job instead of Bobby Robson in 1982 is a far greater debate but Robson, in time, would prove himself as an excellent international manager who understood players and was like a father figure.

If one looks at England's history, the best England managers were not just great man managers and tacticians but they were father figures that understood younger talented players and could nurture them. This is why Ramsey, Winterbottom, Mercer, Greenwood and Robson were successful England managers. They were beyond the club game, had been there and done it and cared about their players. In turn the players responded. Even Venables and Erickson fell into this category. Capello less so as his approach was based less on being a caring father figure who could relate to the players, but was more of a tough disciplinarian.

In England, the manager was more than just a coach. Just as with the clubs, the great managers such as Shankly, Clough, Paisley, Revie, and Nicholson were almost from an earlier age, as they did act like feudal lords and had complete control. The players understood that the manager was "the lord" and expected to be led. Managers, therefore, had to be father-like figures that could communicate effectively with their teams. With England, the manager had to stand taller than the club game, which is why Ramsey and Mercer – and later Greenwood – were successful.

Of course, it was more complex than this but it is no coincidence that Revie, Graham Taylor and Steve McLaren all struggled and ultimately failed to qualify for major tournaments. They were too close to the club game. They tried to bring their club ideals and discipline into the England set up and it just did not work effectively.

It is an interesting debate as to whether the FA should have appointed a manager – a candidate such as Revie – or been more radical and selected a coach. There were some excellent coaches in the game and maybe the FA should have looked a more continental style system where there was a General Manager/Director with a coach directing the players. If one wanted a coach, Malcolm Allison and Dave Sexton could have brought a different dimension to the set up. More logically, the partnership of Mercer and Allison could have been exactly what the FA needed – this may not have been possible – but Mercer and Sexton could have been an exciting combination.

Would it have happened? No. Firstly, it would not have been considered, as the manager – in football – was solely responsible and accountable. Secondly, it was still not accepted the problems were as deep as they were and thirdly, it would have been seen to be an expensive investment.

In 1974, The FA acted too fast. Yes they were decisive and after Ramsey's dismissal, quickly targeted the manager of England's most feared team. There was a simple logic to the move. England, though, was in need of care and nurturing. It would have been better to let Mercer continue with work for at least another two years. History may then have been very different.

"To make matters more difficult, the FA were not even united in their choice. Hardaker was known to dislike Revie and he was an influential figure who could make life difficult for the new manager."

"Revie was unconcerned. He was excited by the new challenge that had presented itself. Hardaker though was not an easy man especially if not onside and Revie could be a very sensitive character. It seems strange to look back, as so much if the time had been taken, stood out to suggest that Revie's appointment was a great risk. He split opinion amongst players and it would be difficult to win some over. He was never going to a unifying source. Leeds did play in a no-nonsense, cynical and professional style at times. He was a man that liked total control and he could be very sensitive and the England job was always going to expose those two vulnerabilities."

"Hardaker, who was described over the years as "the great dictator," "football's godfather," "a cross between Cagney and Caligula," "the League's answer to Idi Amin," and "St Alan of St Annes," reigned supreme as Secretary of the Football League from 1957 to 1979. His successor, Graham Kelly, confirmed "Hardaker loathed Revie with a vengeance that can only have been reserved for a fellow Yorkshireman who he felt had twisted his way to the top". He was an opinionated and arrogant autocrat who saw the Football League as his personal plaything and went out of his way to make life difficult for Leeds United and Don Revie for reasons best known to himself."

The Definitive History of Leeds United.47

England did not need friction behind the scenes but a united approach. England hoped for a fresh start, but before Revie had even started the scale of the mountain had just become higher – to succeed, he not to just win matches but also win over some of his new players and some within the FA. It was less than ideal.

---

47   The Mighty Mighty Whites. (2014) *Don Revie – Part 8 Disgrace and despair (1977-89)*. [Online] Available from: http://www.mightyleeds.co.uk/ managers/revie8.htm [Accessed: 21 November 2014].

"How bad did I feel after the match? Very bad. So bad that I found myself not thinking about football at all for almost a month and that is seriously bad."

Tom.[48]

Focus Group – London, March 2014.

9.

THE REVIE YEARS - 1974-77

Many assumed that Revie would build an England in the image of his Leeds teams and naturally have a bias towards the Leeds players, but in fact Revie's early selections showed a clear objectivity, little bias and a real attacking intent. It was said, somewhat cruelly, that Revie had left Leeds without a backwards glance but maybe he was just excited by the challenge that England presented and felt that he had taken Leeds as far he could. This argument's flaw is that three years later he left England with equal swiftness, but in 1974 he was brave and bold with his selections playing some exciting younger talent in his first year such as the QPR Captain Gerry Francis, the QPR Wing Dave Thomas, Alan Hudson, and the Newcastle striker Malcolm Macdonald.

The first year of Revie's reign offered genuine glimpses of a new beginning. In his first match, England defeated Czechoslovakia 3–0. His second was a disappointing home draw with Portugal (0–0) but real hope came in the shape of the World Champions, West Germany, and visiting Wembley in early 1975. Revie greeted the World Champions with a new captain in the experienced Alan Ball and an attacking line up. It was England's 100th match at Wembley Stadium and the midfield trio of Ball, Hudson and Bell dominated the match. In attack, Revie played the ever reliable Channon alongside Keegan and Macdonald and they carried real threat to the German defence – especially Macdonald who's pace seemed to trouble the experienced West Germans. England won through goals from Bell and Macdonald and with this victory, English hearts believed once again.

The year continued with a victory at Wembley over Cyprus (with Macdonald scoring all five goals) and in Cyprus (1–0). At the end of the Home Championships, England drew against Northern Ireland (0–0) in Belfast and Wales (2–2) at Wembley before exploding against the Scots with a 5–1 victory, which launched Gerry Francis as a new national hero.

Gerry Francis was the leader of the exciting QPR team that was challenging in the English League and came, in 1976, so close to winning the title. Francis was a direct running, forceful player that would lead from the front. Revie saw the qualities in Francis that he wanted for his captain to take England forward. He would win 12 caps for England with eight being as Captain. Francis promised so much and yet his career was undermined by injury.

But the first year was to prove to be a mirage. Revie would chop and change and seemed to become uncertain. It was a strange for a club manager that he would not let a team just grow and evolve naturally. By the end of his first year as manager, Revie was already onto his third captain. He started with Hughes for the early matches, and then selected the last of the World Cup winning captains before selecting Francis to lead him into his second year.

If anything, it showed that Revie was not sure in his own mind as to his best team and there was a lack of consistency in his thinking. Ball was dropped after the 5–1 thrashing of Scotland and yet he had done a fine job in bringing stability to the team in the first year. Francis was still a new face with great potential but had not been a regular player. It would have made sense to continue with Ball at least for another year. Of course, one could argue that Revie wanted to rebuild the team quickly, but there was a change after the first year's promise. He seemed to begin to distrust the naturally skilled players and rely on the tough, solid, no-nonsense players from the league.

It was this change in Revie's mind-set that is crucial to understand because throughout he would pick the "flair" players but he rarely gave them enough time to settle and grow.

There was friction in Revie's England as he tried to bring the approach that had worked for him so well with Leeds to the England set up, but he just didn't translate. Revie wanted to create Club England – and many others have tried – but the players were never together long enough. At the same time, it was rumoured that he would be so detailed about the opposition that the players would feel they had too much information. Again this was natural. Revie was a meticulous planner and the length of time between matches meant that Revie could study the opposition and plan in depth. The problem was that the players didn't share the same time nor inclination. This, in turn, created friction and one can understand why Revie would grow exasperated and seek to work with those that he could trust. The problem was that the team he built, by 1977, did possess the best players in England at its core.

Revie's biggest match was arguably in Rome in November 1976 against Italy. This was a World Cup qualifying game and England had to at least draw. The team selected included good players that were not of international calibre – players such as Dave Clement, Trevor Cherry, Brian Greenhoff and Stan Bowles. Bowles had come in for this match as he had been displaying some sparkling and skilful play for QPR, but he was not an experienced international for a testing arena such as Rome's Olympic Stadium and he was not used to playing with either Keegan or Channon. Cherry and Greenhoff were excellent club holding players. One can argue for a long time as to whether they were of international quality or not – there will be split opinions – but neither were attacking midfielders. England's formation that day could be read as 4-2-1-3. It was simply not balanced. Brooking was the one creative midfielder and his role would be to create for Bowles, Keegan and Channon. The Italians were, at the time, renowned for their defensive ability and they would not have been intimidated by three attackers supported by one creative midfielder. It presented the Italians with the tactical initiative and they accepted, as England lost bravely 2–0 to goals from Antognoni and a great diving header from Roberto Bettega.

The game cried out less for the flair of a Stan Bowles, who would be left isolated as centre-forward but another creative midfielder such as a Tony Currie, or Alan Hudson. (Francis was injured.)

In the next game against Holland the line up was arguably even worse. It read:

Clemence, Clement, Watson, Doyle, Madeley, Beattie, Greenhoff, Bowles, Brooking Francis, and Keegan.

The Dutch easily won the match and again one can easily see why. The formation again would have been 4-2-1-3 but this time with no real recognised left-back. Beattie could play there but was more a central-defender. Mike Doyle was a great club player (and captain) but was not of international calibre. Brooking again was left isolated and worse there were two highly skilled players in Bowles and Francis who were as skilful as the Dutch, but were left stranded. In Italy one could make an argument for a defensive approach but at home – at Wembley – against the Dutch? What happened to English bulldog spirit? It was just tactically naive to play three attackers with two holding midfielders. There was a great statistic from the game, which showed that Cruyff touched the ball 61 times – twice as many as any England player.

Kevin Beattie would later say:

"They ripped us to pieces that night. I only played nine times for England but that was easily the worst game. Cruyff was unbelievable. They just passed the ball so quickly, all the way through the team from back to front."

"We couldn't get near them and even Don Revie afterwards admitted they had played some smashing stuff. It was Total Football and, although on one hand it was just awful, you really had to admire it. I've no idea why I'm flat out for the goal. I must have been having a lie-down. I'd been marking Robbie Rensenbrink and he'd tired me out."[49]

Trevor Francis who made his debut in that match commented: "I had waited a long time to make my international debut and was thrilled when Don Revie chose me to play. It wasn't the greatest of starts for me, but I know I won't be alone when I say it was no disgrace on this particular occasion because that Dutch team contained some very special players.

"People ask about Total Football, and what it was like to play against, in practice."

"The fact was that this was the first time that players were expected to be comfortable in possession, regardless of where they stood on the pitch. That was a novelty. It hadn't been seen before. They were also supposed to interchange their

49   *Daily Mail.* (2012) *The night Total Football conquered Wembley thanks to Cruyff and his Orange masters.* [Online] Available from: http://www.dailymail. co.uk/sport/football/article-2107856/England-v-Holland-Remember-1977-Total-Football-conquered-Wembley.html [Accessed: 21 November 2014].

position and be intelligent enough to realise what was going on around them."

"I would go so far as to say there were three who you could term as world-class. Even now, when you are talking about the greats of the game, they would have to be discussed. Certainly, that went for Cruyff. He was the best player in Europe at that time. He was the one player I tried to model parts of my own game upon."

"His speed with the ball that night was terrific. And he had this knack of almost slowing to a standstill. It would lull the defender into a false sense of security. Almost like that nothing was happening, that he was stuck for an idea. Then he would explode into action. He had great pace from a standing start."

"I also tried to copy the move that became known as the Cruyff turn'. I practised it relentlessly."

England were left knowing that they were not competing at the top table and were struggling to find their way to compete.

So where did it change for Revie? He had selected boldly in his first year, so what did go wrong?

Clearly in the 1975–76 season and most probably with the defeat in Czechoslovakia, which meant that England would not qualify for the European Championships of 76. Revie had set his stall out to rebuild England and he had failed at the first attempt. Revie was a man driven to prove himself and this failure would have hurt him. However it also changed him and changed England for the worse.

England opened the 75–76 season with a victory in Switzerland – 2–1 and went to Czechoslovakia in good spirits and the team that Revie choose was attacking and full of purpose:

Clemence, Todd, McFarland, Gilliard, Madeley, Francis (capt), Bell, Channon, Keegan, Clarke and Macdonald.

How different was this team in attitude and approach to the one that would play against the Italians a year later?

One could argue the team could line up as 4-3-3, 4-2-2-2 or even 4-2-4 with two midfielders that were real box-to-box players that loved to attack the opposition. The team boasted four attackers with two exceptional strikers in Clarke and Macdonald. This was an aggressive set up and very positive in intent. One could argue that, if anything, it was too aggressive – the exact opposite to the structure of the teams for Italy (1976) and Holland (1977) and that it did need a holding midfield player instead of two out and out strikers and two inside-forwards.

England started well in the game and opened the scoring with Channon on 26 minutes. All seemed to be going well before they let in two sloppy goals either side of half-time on 45 mins and 47 mins from Nehoda and Gallis. However, England did not lie down and they fired back and Keegan scored with a diving header from a free kick. It was ruled offside but TV would later prove Keegan had been on side.

England lost 2–1 but the score should have been 2–2. It was unfortunate. Even more unfortunate as the actual match had been started the day before in thick fog and had to be abandoned after 17 minutes with England in control. As with the Poland match, it did seem the Gods were not giving England any breaks in competitive games, but the real problem was that Revie's mind-set was beginning to change and become more defensive.

Don Revie was a complicated man. He was born in Middle-borough, North Yorkshire in 1927. His mother sadly died from cancer in 1939 when he was only 12 years old. It was a difficult time for the young boy but he loved football and devoted his time to learning the game. In 1944, he joined Leicester City. In 1949, he became Captain of the team and the team did well having a great run in the FA Cup that took them to the Final. However, Revie suffered a nasal haemorrhage caused by a burst vein one week before the Final. The condition became so severe it would threaten his life and see him miss his first chance to play at Wembley. Revie was massively disappointed and soon left the club to join first Hull City, then Manchester City where he played 162 games in five years, scoring 37 goals. He had scored 25 goals in 96 games for Leicester. In 1954–55, Revie would play for England six times, scoring four goals. He was also the Football Writers Footballer of the Year in 1955 and won the FA Cup in 56. It was the best time of his career.

However, in 1956, Revie departed for Sunderland then Leeds United whom he joined in 1958. He became player-manager in 1961 and so started the rise of the great Leeds United team which was really founded – just as Sir Alex Ferguson did later with his class of 92 – on his youth players, which included the likes of Norman Hunter, Jimmy Greenhoff, Gary Sprake, Paul Reaney, Paul Madeley, Billy Bremner, Eddie Gray, Terry Cooper and Peter Lorimer. All these players became internationals or played for the leading teams in the league. Revie's great strength was that he built a close-knit culture that really blended well. He was strong on discipline and was a tough, no nonsense manager, which worked well with the young players that came through the ranks.

In the 13 years, Revie managed Leeds United, they won two Football League First Division titles, one FA Cup, one League Cup, two Inter-Cities Fairs Cup titles, one Football League Second Division title and one Charity Shield. He also steered them to three more FA Cup Finals, two FA Cup semi-finals, one more Inter-Cities Fairs Cup Final, one Fairs Cup semi-final, one European Cup semi-final, one Cup Winners' Cup Final and five runners up places in the league.

It was a phenomenal record and the Leeds team will always go down as one of the great club sides of any era. The names of Lorimer, Clarke, Bremner, Hunter, Gray lived with almost every football mad child in England. Leeds were the team to beat. They were respected but they were not loved. This was because they were seen to be having a culture that meant they had to win at all costs – even if it meant breaking the rules. Leeds could play some wonderful football, but they used would play cynically and aggressively if needs be. Many of the great purists disliked Leeds and Revie. They often felt that Leeds were too good to need to lower themselves to bad behaviour and should strive to be less cynical in approach – but it was a culture that Revie had built where winning appeared to be prime objective.

This was made worse by allegations made in later years of bribery and intimidation. Both the *Daily Mirror* and *Sunday People* claimed that Revie had attempted to bribe Wolverhampton Wanderers players to lose a crucial match in May 1972. The papers quoted Wolves midfielder Danny Hegan and former Leeds United goalkeeper Gary Sprake's claims that Revie's captain Billy Bremner had tried to arrange a bribe. Bremner sued for libel and won £100,000 libel damages, along with legal costs, after both Hegan and Sprake refused to repeat their allegations under oath in court. Wolves player Derek Dougan, who had scored against Leeds in the match in question, testified that no attempt was made to bribe Wolves and that the claims were nonsense.

Additionally Bob Stokoe would later claim that while managing Bury in 1962, Revie had offered him a bribe of £500 to "go easy" on his Leeds side who were at the time struggling against relegation to the Third Division and that he had become enraged when Revie responded to his refusal to accept the bribe by asking, "in that case, may I speak to your players?"[50]

Given all this as the background, and it must have been well known behind closed doors, it does make the decision to appoint Revie a strange one. Look at the facts:

1. Leeds United had been built through the development of the youth players combined with a number of experienced pros (such as John Charles, Johnny Giles, Bobby Collins) and a strong club culture, which was controlled by Revie. This was admirable for a club built over years but would not work in the international arena.

2. Leeds were seen to be an intimidating, cynical team. Was this the right type of background for England – especially as a successor for Sir Alf Ramsey who was the ethical, well man-nered and polite?

3. Even though the allegations came out later, they were rumours and the FA should logically have looked into these before appointing. England was already in a period of distress.

---

50   The Mighty Mighty Whites. (2014) *Don Revie – Part 8 Disgrace and despair (1977-89.)* [Online] Available from: http://www.mightyleeds.co.uk/ managers/revie8.htm [Accessed: 21 November 2014].

Surely it could not run any risk of something coming out that would blacken the good name of England?

4. There were some very good managers that would have been good appointments – even Joe Mercer who was in situ or the Young Bobby Robson who was building a great team at Ipswich (and who would become manager just eight years later), Ron Greenwood or Brian Clough. With all this talent and knowledge there, why would you choose a man known for his toughness. Greenwood's West Ham was widely respected for its football and had developed the West Ham Three – Moore, Hurst and Peters.

5. Leeds United divided opinion. Of course, this would naturally mean the knives of the critics would never be far away. In any rebuilding process, time is needed and it is always harder with critics ready and waiting. Revie had critics in football circles, within clubs, within the FA and in the newspapers. For a direct honest man, this was difficult.

It is always harsh to criticise a man after the event and Revie was a good footballing man. To place things into context, some would fairly argue that a win at all costs mentality was what England needed. And in fairness his early teams were exciting sides.

No, the problem lay in what changed Revie's approach from the attacking intent of 1975 to the caution of 1976.

Some say that there were a number of reasons. Firstly he began to lose the confidence within the FA and that Revie and Sir Harold Thompson, Chairman of the FA, were often at loggerheads. Thompson was even rumoured to try and influence selection. Secondly, he began to lose the players with his large dossiers on the opposition, which served to disengage the players. If Revie felt that the players were not responding or listening to his briefings, it could explain the change in approach and the change towards a defensive cautious approach.

Finally, Revie had developed at Leeds a 'win at all costs' mentality. Failure to qualify in 1976 would have hurt him deeply. His mind-set was that of winning. The problem with the England job is not just that failure is so high profile, but that one has to wait and dwell on the failure for months before the next game. In club football, you can take one's frustration out with a game that will invariably follow shortly after any disappointment. In international football, the opposite is true and this is where Revie may have struggled most. He loved nothing more than being the leader of an "extended" family of players and he was highly effective in this role – but this was not the international set up, which was more of a mix of talented rival players who would come together for just a few days. This needed a very different managerial approach and someone who could unite players quickly and with ease. This was not Revie. Robson, Greenwood, Mercer and even Clough would have been more easily suited. It was always rumoured that Clough was not the most intense manager and could bring teams together with little time invested.

The real change in Revie after the failure to qualify for the 1976 Europeans first showed itself in the match versus Wales in March 1976 with the following team selection:

Clemence, Neal, Doyle, Thompson, Mills, Cherry, Kennedy, Brooking, Boyer, Keegan, Channon.[51]

The team won 2–1 but the selection include players that were not the best in their positions in the country and were arguably not of international calibre – Boyer, Doyle, Cherry, Kennedy.

---

51   http://www.11v11.com/teams/england/tab/matches/season/1977

Ray Kennedy had been one of Arsenal's forwards in the double team of 1971 but had converted to midfield with Liverpool. He was a good player who could attack and defend. There was some logic and could provide some balance. But just as with Ramsey, failure seemed to mean that the reaction was to throw out some of the good as well as what had not worked.

England's next match was against Wales again in May and Revie introduced Brian Greenhoff, Tony Towers, Stuart Pearson, and Peter Taylor. Were these international players or excellent club players? It did suggest Revie was searching for answers.

For the big match against Scotland at Hampden, Revie's team was;[52]

Clemence, Mills, Todd, McFarland, Thompson, Kennedy, Francis (capt), Taylor, Keegan, Channon, Pearson.

What is interesting about Revie's teams throughout is that he seems to leave the midfield vulnerable, or maybe he was seeking to do an English version of the Dutch's Total Football approach, where the midfield and attack worked closely together? The Dutch had won many admirers with their approach and it was certainly effective. This would, in practical terms, mean that players would need to adapt more from their club systems to a much more flexible approach with Keegan and Channon playing both midfield and attack. It would certainly explain why Revie was attracted to the flexible players such as Ray Kennedy, Brian Greenhoff, Paul Madeley, Trevor Cherry and later Brian Talbot. The problem was that they were versatile for a reason and they were not experts in a single role.

The argument against Revie at the time was that he would over

---

52   http://www.11v11.com/teams/england/tab/matches/season/1977

brief players and leave them confused and that it would have been better to rely on simple systems that related to the player's clubs and which they could easily relate to – ie playing the players to their strengths. Maybe Revie had a vision for what he wanted to achieve in a style of play but could not find the personnel to achieve it?

Wherever the truth lay, Revie's team often lost the midfield battles and as a result, the strike force was never as potent as it could or should have been.

There is an old saying and apologies, – "There is nothing better than good sex and nothing worse than bad sex". It is the same with football. Football is about a good defence coupled with a creative midfield/wings plus great strikers. Revie so often asked Brooking to do too much and left the strikers isolated. England football had been used to "good sex" for years and now the play had become the "bad sex". Of course, this is mildly silly but it makes the point. There was little imagination in England's play. England had a team that had made the country proud during the Ramsey and Winterbottom years. Yes, 1973 had gone wrong but the 1976 and 1977 England teams were a sorry reflection of what had gone before. England was at a low ebb and were selecting players that were honest, brave and true, but not the ones that would challenge the great teams. Where was the creative flair within the team to unlock organised defences, to make other teams scared of England as they once were? It was asking the world-class players to perform heroics and of course it did not happen.

Against Scotland at Hampden, England lost 2–1 to an unfortunate goal when Clemence let Dalglish's shot through his legs but the Scots overran the English midfield and were the better team. In fairness, the attacking intent was still there but Pearson, Taylor, Kennedy were not of the level to face a Scottish team enjoying their Golden era. The 1978 Scottish team was even considered to be a good outside bet for the 1978 World Cup and the England team lacked the depth and experience – even if the winning goal was fortunate.

England went on a summer tour to the USA to play Brazil, Italy and Team America and they played well. They lost by a single goal to Brazil. An experimental team (which included a debut for the talented Ray Wilkins) beat Italy 3–2 in New York after being 2–0 down and then they beat a Team America, which included Bobby Moore, 3–1.

A team was coming together but the problem was that the team seemed to be a mix of the best and good club players and at the highest levels this would always leave a team vulnerable and England did struggle.

After the defeat in Italy, it was always a matter of time before a change would take place. England needed some elusive luck to be able to qualify and for a proud man such as Revie to face the inevitable sack should England fail to qualify for the 1978 World Cup Finals, it was natural that he sought a way out. Much is made of Revie's resignation as a betrayal and a cowardly act. This is all too harsh. This was simply a proud man who did not wish to suffer the indignity of the sack. What was wrong was the way Revie went about it? Revie accepted the position as coach to the United Arab Emirates and leaked the news to the *Daily Mail* before the FA formally received his resignation. It is hard to explain Revie's behaviour at this time, bar there must have been some anger within him at the FA, but it all became a PR disaster for the man and worse than if had faced the sack. He looked like he was running away and taking a lucrative contract (worth £340,000) rather than face the consequences of the team's results.

The FA suspended Revie from football for 10 years on a charge of bringing the game into disrepute. Revie contested his suspension in a lawsuit against the FA, and the court overturned the suspension. After leaving the UAE coaching role in 1980 he took over management of Al-Nasr, followed in 1984 by the Egyptian club Al-Ahly of Cairo.

This must have felt like exile to a man that only four years earlier had seen his Leeds United team start a 29 match unbeaten run that took them to the Championship in 74. This is a man that lived and breathed club football, but rather than accepting his failings at international level, left what he loved behind for financial security and football that could never be as he had known. It is hard to defend. Revie was a genuine footballing heavyweight, but his reputation will always be tarnished not by how England struggled on the field but by the allegations against him and how he resigned from a prestigious role as England manager.

As the definitive history of Leeds United explains:[53]

"Ever since England's defeat in a vital World Cup qualifying game against Italy in Rome in November 1976, there had been the air of a man on borrowed time about manager Don Revie. He was convinced that the FA were building up to his dismissal, and the clever money in the newspapers was on the axe falling after the Wembley return against the Italians completed the group stages."

"The paranoia which had been building up in Revie's troubled mind finally got the better of him, and he decided to deny

---

53   The Mighty Mighty Whites. (2014) *Don Revie – Part 8 Disgrace and despair. (1977-89)* [Online] Available from: http://www.mightyleeds.co.uk/ managers/revie8.htm [Accessed: 21 November 2014].

his masters the satisfaction of sacking him, and determined
the timing and manner of his own departure after securing
a lucrative role as supremo of football in the United Arab
Emirates."

The way he chose to break the story led to one of the most histrionic
and self-righteous newspaper campaigns of all time. Revie sold the
story of his departure to the *Daily Mail*. On 11 July 1977, the paper
scooped Fleet Street with a front-page story in which Revie poured
out his heart:

> "I sat down with Elsie one night and we agreed that the job
> was no longer worth the aggravation. It was bringing too
> much heartache to those nearest to us. Nearly everyone in
> the country seems to want me out. So I am giving them what
> they want. I know people will accuse me of running away
> and it does sicken me that I cannot finish the job by taking
> England to the World Cup Finals in Argentina next year. But
> the situation has become impossible."

The FA were furious, especially as they did not receive Revie's letter
of resignation until later that morning. The manner of his leaving
rankled with the pompous patriots of Fleet Street who responded to
public antipathy by hastening Revie's fall from grace, branding him a
traitor. Some of the articles written were hysterical in the extreme and
old enemy Bob Stoke said bluntly, "He should have been castrated for
the way he left England," while Alan Hardaker's voice was thick with
biting sarcasm as he spitefully snapped, "Don Revie's decision doesn't
surprise me in the slightest. Now I can only hope he can quickly learn
to call out bingo numbers in Arabic."

Undoubtedly, Revie's handling of events was clumsy and served to give ammunition for his critics' most bile-ridden, venomous out-pourings. Even the more considered comments pointed out the flaws.

Johnny Giles: "It's obvious he shouldn't have done it the way he did. He didn't do himself justice. He left himself open to savage criticism by telling the *Daily Mail* first. There was no defence for it. He ruined a lot of good work and then became a baddy ... which he wasn't. But who isn't greedy? The people who write the stories in the tabloid newspapers might be the greediest in the world."

Gerald Sinstadt gave a cool headed and objective assessment of matters in *The Times* on 15 July:[54]

"Once again the England football team is manager less. Don Revie ... has resigned without waiting for the virtually inev-itable failure to qualify for the 1978 Finals. His task, already difficult in a period when the general standard was mediocre, had been made harder by injury to several players who might have raised the level. To that extent Mr Revie was entitled to sympathy. Now, with the timing and the manner of his depar-ture, that sympathy and more will vanish."

"It is nevertheless remarkable that the conduct of the out-going manager has so far attracted more comment than the qualifications of those who might take his place. For this Mr Revie himself is largely to blame. The first announcement – to his employers, the Football Association, as well as to the

---

54   The Definitive History of Leeds United http://www.mightyleeds.co.uk/managers/revie8.htm

public at large – came in the *Daily Mail.* He was leaving, Mr Revie was reported to have said, to protect his family from the criticism his job increasingly attracted: 'It was bringing too much heartache.'"

"Twenty-four hours later, the *Daily Mail* was able to reveal that the heartache had been eased by an offer to run football in the United Arab Emirates for the next four years with a remuneration of £340,000 tax-free. It was also disclosed that when Mr Revie abandoned his team for the first match of the recent tour of South America in order to watch Finland play Italy in England's World Cup qualifying group, he also took the opportunity to visit Dubai."

"Although some of the response to these developments may be attributed to Fleet Street pique, the issues lie deeper than professional envy in the media. Whether the *Daily Mail* out-smarted its rivals as a result of the perspicacity of its football correspondent or the generosity of its accountants can be only a matter of conjecture. Whichever the explanation, either was certain to expose Mr Revie to more of the criticism he has apparently found so burdensome."

"As manager of England, Mr Revie involved – and, indeed, sought to involve – the whole nation in his public responsi-bilities of the past three years. He might therefore have felt obliged to end that involvement with a more generously open announcement, especially in the light of his stated resentment of the fact that 'everyone seems to have believed that I've just been feathering my own nest.'"

"The timing of the resignation is another matter. Those who have been forecasting England's certain failure to qualify for a place in Argentina next year can hardly claim that Revie would have enhanced the prospects by remaining in office. The sequel to England's matches against Luxembourg (12 October) and Italy (16 November) was expected to be a clamour for Mr Revie's removal. So what harm has come from his anticipation of the demand?"

"In Mr Revie's defence it could be said that his position at the Football Association was not, in any case, as secure as it should have been. Although he undeniably had his supporters at Lancaster Gate, he cannot have been unaware of grapevine mutterings last season that unofficial soundings were being made about his possible successor."

"Perhaps it is worth restating the basic facts of the matter. Mr Revie was England's manager for three years and one week. In that time 29 full international matches were played. Fourteen were won, eight drawn and seven lost. More than 50 players were given the chance to prove themselves. This was interpreted as indecision rather than a display of fair treatment, but in reality reflected the paucity of really outstanding individuals."

"Failure in the European Championship, diminishing hopes in the World Cup, and finally humiliation in the home international championship provoked mounting disenchantment among critics, paid and unpaid. At that juncture came the offer of a job, which would guarantee in four years security for life. Which of us can say that, in that position, we would have made a different decision? Mr Revie's weakness, surprisingly, in a man who has worked hard at public relations since he became England's manager, was to make his announcement in a manner that was undignified and ungrateful."

"Team games were nurtured in Britain a century ago as a visible expression of a code of ethics which, roughly speaking, governed the attitudes of society at large. Demonstrably, many of those attitudes have changed. We may deplore the transformation but it is naïve to suppose that sport can indefinitely preserve old standards in isolation."

"Nonetheless, there are qualities which should not lightly be abandoned. It is possible to sympathise with Mr Revie for finding himself weighing in the scales an individual's right to better his own lot against the obligations of one who has taken on the role of keeper of a nation's dreams. Equally, it is impossible to escape the irony of the man who encouraged crowds to sing *Land of Hope and Glory* turning to seek his desserts in the desert."

Revie had spoken of the intolerable pressures placed upon him as England manager, but they were as nothing compared to what followed in the wake of his departure.

The FA charged him with bringing the game into disrepute. Revie refused to attend the hearing in which he was suspended indefinitely from any involvement in FA-controlled football until he appeared to face their complaints. It was 18 December 1978 before Revie would agree to meet.

The eventual hearing commenced with two objections from the accused. Firstly, his counsel argued that the FA had no jurisdiction over their client and, secondly, they objected to the presiding presence of Sir Harold Thompson, whose post as FA Chairman destroyed his impartiality. Both these objections were summarily brushed aside and Don Revie was banned from English football for ten years.

The severity of the judgement prompted Revie to take the case to the High Court a year later. Revie made a claim for damages and demanded that the court declare his ban illegal. The crux of the case hinged upon the hostility of Sir Harold Thompson, whom Revie's barrister described as "prosecutor, witness, judge and jury". The judge listened to a lengthy series of complaints against Thompson, none of which impressed him. He concluded: "Mr Revie is a very prickly man and I think he has been brooding on imagined wrongs". Nevertheless, Mr Justice Cantley quashed the ten-year ban, although his summing up was scathing:

> "Mr Revie was the English team manager. He held the highest post of its kind in English professional football and he published and presented to the public a sensational and notorious example of disloyalty, breach of duty, discourtesy and selfishness. His conduct brought English professional football, at a high level, into disrepute."

The FA was ordered to pay one third of Revie's costs plus the entirety of their own. Ted Croker estimated that their total losses were in the region of £141,000.

Lord Harewood: "I think it was an agony for him and the elements of character assassination on the part of the defending counsel grilling him were very unattractive. The summing-up of the judge was one of the craziest things I have ever read. I think that judge was extremely ill versed in human behaviour … he was an ass. If he really thought that Sir Harold Thompson had behaved admirably and Don hadn't, then he is a very, very poor judge of character ... and of evidence. He plainly disbelieved every word I said but I don't give a bugger what he thought."

Ted Croker: "I didn't like the way Cantley handled it at all. I thought his summing-up was very wrong, his assessment of the various characters totally wrong ... he praised Sir Harold Thompson to the hilt as being an honourable man. I didn't think it was fair and he should not have worried so much about the personalities."

Looking back at the sorry episode, it is difficult to avoid the conclusion that Revie was simply myopic and self-destructive. He clearly underestimated the depth of ill-feeling provoked by his abrupt desertion and as a result suffered terrible damage to his reputation. Ironically, it was all so unnecessary. His detractors maintained that greed played the major part in hastening his departure, but the actual timing was not particularly clever in financial terms. If he had stayed with England for those vital last months he might even have won everything – the Arab money, compensation from the FA and a relatively quiet exit.

In the end Revie served out three years of the four that the United Arab Emirates had signed him for, with his new bosses terminating his contract in May 1980 by mutual agreement, on the pretext that an Arabic-speaking coach was required. Elsie had never settled in the

Middle East, but Revie enjoyed considerable success, noting, "We lost only one of our last nine games at national level. I am leaving a squad of good young players and am very happy about the whole business."

Although the news of his resignation caused outrage for fair reason, it also did generate a sense of relief, as England were not playing good football under Revie. That's the irony – Revie could have resigned with honour and probably have found a return to club football with a good team. Of course, he may have reasoned that he could not achieve again what he did with Leeds. In truth, it does not matter. He left with a cloud over his name but overall, it was the right thing to happen. The sadness was that Revie arguably never the right man to lead England. The comparison with the dignity of Ramsey's[1] departure told its own story. England not only had lost three years, they were a worse team too.

To counter this view, the fair question to ask is what team should Revie had sent out onto the field and what formation? Defenders of Revie will argue that England did not possess world-class players and he was handicapped by injury and average players.

Firstly, it seems strange that England possesses such average players just three years after it could boast so many players to choose from. It also seems a strange defence when one considers Liverpool won the European Cup in 1977 and would defend a year later. Nottingham Forest would then win the European Cup in 79 and 80.

So what is the truth?

Maybe let's start with a number of questions:

- Malcolm Macdonald played 14 times for England and scored six goals – five being in one match. He did retire early at the age of 29 but this was in 1979. Most would argue that Super-mac – as Macdonald was nicknamed – was better than Stuart Pearson. Why was he dropped by Revie?

- Bob Latchford was arguably the best old-fashioned centre-forward in England – why was he never selected until Greenwood took over?

- As stated, Revie did play attacking formations but rarely with wingers. His formations would be narrow and yet Manchester United from 76–79 boasted an exciting team with two great wingers in Gordon Hill and Steve Coppell. Coppell would go on to become a regular under Greenwood.

- England possesses some exceptional younger talent that would come through over the next few years – Laurie Cunningham, Gordon Cowans, Billy Bonds, Peter Barnes, Ray Wilkins, Glenn Hoddle, Steve Wicks, Bryan Robson and a young Garth Crooks. Bar Wilkins, the others were not nurtured by Revie's senior squad. Hoddle was already singled out in 1976 to be a talent that could light up England's midfield; although still very raw, Robson was in the West Brom team with Cunningham.

- Revie became overly defensive and relied on holding players. In 1977, England toured South America earning three creditable draws but the teams possessed little flair. Against Brazil, Argentina and Uruguay the midfield was, Brian Talbot, Brian Greenhoff, and Ray Wilkins. If only England had employed either some width or flair.

So, for debating purposes, how about this England squad for 1977 from players that did not play for England's first team:

Goal: Peter Shilton, Joe Corrigan
Defence: John Gidman, Billy Bonds, Tommy Smith, David Nish, Paul Reaney, Frank Lampard, Derek Statham, Stephen Wicks.
Midfield: Tony Currie, Alan Hudson, Glenn Hoddle, Steve Coppell, Gordon Hill, Graham Paddock, Bryan Robson. Gordon Cowans, Dennis Mortimer
Attack: Malcolm Macdonald, Bob Latchford, Tony Woodcock, Eric Gates, Laurie Cuningham, Duncan McKenzie.

When one considers the calibre of these players and add in Allan Clarke, Martin Peters, Mike Pejic, Martin Dobson, Ian Callaghan, and Terry McDermott who were all playing good football, then it is clear that the talent was available. Some of the above players, in the alternative squad should have been in England's squad or certainly being introduced.

- Billy Bonds was the leader of West Ham, who won the FA Cup in 1975. He was strong, a driving force.
- Frank Lampard was a talented left-back.
- Duncan McKenzie was an exceptional talent with so much ability.
- Laurie Cunningham. Gordon Hill, Steve Coppell and Peter Barnes were wingers that could have given Revie's teams width.
- Graham Paddock had been one of the driving forces and threats with West Ham's surge to the European Cup Winners' Cup Final of 1976.

- Tony Currie and Hudson could both have brought skill and craft to midfield. (Hoddle was clearly for the future.)

Now imagine the team of:

Revie's X1:   Clemence, Neal, Mills, Watson, Hughes, Cherry, Talbot, Brooking, Channon, Keegan, Pearson.

Versus

Alternative: Shilton, Gidman, Bonds (capt), Wicks, Lampard, Currie, Robson, Paddock, Coppell, Cunningham, Latchford.

It would be a great game of energy and flair versus defensive stalwarts. I suspect the game would hinge on how the two wingers in Coppell and Cunningham would have fared against Revie's defensive combinations.

How about the winner take on:

Alternative 2: Corrigan, Reaney, Nish, Smith, Pejic, Dobson, Peters (capt), McDermott, Hudson, Macdonald, McKenzie.

One can debate endlessly but the point it proves is that the talent has always been there for England in abundance. It was still a question of management, structure and framework. These problems would persist but England also needed someone who understood international football, someone who understood the tactics of the top teams and someone who understood talented players – Enter Ron Greenwood.

"Peter Storey was known as the bastard's bastard. The hard men in the league teams were brutal. Ruthless. They would not care if they broke a player's leg. It was said teams would target George Best with the aim of taking him out of the game in almost every time he played. can you imagine? You would need to be bloody brave to just go onto the pitch knowing that someone wanted to break your leg just to win a game of football. It cant have been any fun being a skilful player in those days. I do wonder what Best would have achieved if he had been Dutch and played alongside Cruyff and Nesskens? Imagine Best in the World Cup Final in 74 with the skills he had. He was born in the right era; just wrong country."

(Tommy)[55]

10.

'Pass Me If You Can'
- The Hard Men that Led England's Clubs.

The infrastructure and administration of the English game may have had its flaws and the England manager may not have made the right choice in either selections or tactics, but the counter argument is that the game is still about players and good players should be able to adapt to any given environment. If only … international football required far more depth to the process for success to be achieved.

There is little doubt that, as the world praised and applauded the skills of the Dutch and West Germans teams of the mid 1970s, the English game was dominated by a group of tough characters that formed the back lines for many of England's clubs and also led the club sides themselves.

If one looked at the captains that led England's leading teams, there were few proven world-class players in the group but there were many central defenders who were natural leaders, whose leadership styles were based on their physicality, which was more prominent than their natural technical skill. It is, of course, too simplistic to describe these men as killing any creative flair in the game, but they certainly believed in intimidation and raw power. There are few sports that thrive when intimidation is dominant but in the 1970s this was certainly the case and it was matched by the intensity and raw emotion seen on the terraces.

The list of the league's hard men were household names as much as the ones of the international players. It was the era when any skilful player needed to be not afraid of a highly physical approach. As

European football developed a high intensity passing games, British football was focused upon never letting a creative player have the time on the ball to hurt a team. One can argue that English football had become too brutal and this was matched by the violence on the terraces over the 70s.

In the early 1970s, George Best was the league's most talented player and in terms of skill, he matched the very best players in the world. In the early 70s his career began to come off the rails. Yes, he played life fast and loose with drink and women but he loved football, loved Manchester United and yet would go missing for days and weeks, in the early 70s George Best became a soap opera alone. Of course the drink, adulation and desire for women were his areas of vulnerability but is it any wonder he looked for escapism, as this was a shy man that became a target of every hard man in every team in the land. There are many video clips of Best as he hurdles one mistimed tackle after another. His skill was avoiding have being taken out and still showing moments of pure brilliance.

Yes, George Best caused his own downfall, but the game also made it as hard as possible for him to grow into the world class player almost everyone who watched him knew that he could have been. Many believe he was equally as skilled as Cruyff. Maybe. The difference was that Cruyff was self-disciplined and lived a life within set guidelines to maximise his potential. Best did anything but. It does tell its own story.

Is this making excuses for George Best? As a point for comparison, it is worth noting that the great Liverpool manager reputedly turned Ray Kennedy from a forward into a midfielder because he believed Kennedy had lost his appetite for forward play when defenders were constantly using negative tactics. Kennedy had been a rising young forward with Arsenal when they won the Double in 1971 and was seen to be destined for a great career. He did have a great career with Liverpool and England but as a midfield player. He was known to be one of the calmest, most laid back of characters so it does tell a story that he had grown weary of the defensive approach in his twenties.

Soccer's Hard Men, (a 1992 video), featured footage of British players known for their ferocity and included Graeme Souness, Bryan Robson, Nobby Stiles, Norman Hunter, Jack Charlton, Steve McMahon, Tommy Smith, Peter Storey, Ron "Chopper Harris" and Billy Bremner. It is no coincidence that only one player did not play in the 70s.

In fairness, there had always been tough men in the game – players that would mix the physical with genuine footballing skill. This was nothing new but the difference was these players had also become the leaders of their clubs and of course, it was bound to influence the environment and those emerging.

Just for a moment, set these players aside and consider others that played with physicality from that era:

-   Joe Jordan (Leeds and Manchester Utd)
-   Willie Young (Spurs and Arsenal)
-   Jimmy Case (Liverpool)
-   Duncan Forbes (Norwich City)
-   Mike England (Spurs)
-   Gordon McQueen (Leeds and Man Utd)
-   Peter Storey (Arsenal)
-   Peter Simpson (Arsenal)
-   Brian Greenhoff (Man Utd and Leeds Utd)
-   Jack Charlton (Leeds Utd)
-   Graeme Souness (Middlesborough and Liverpool)

- Trevor Cherry (Leeds Utd)
- Billy Bonds (West Ham)

It may sound as though the blame for England's fall is being laid at the feet of the hard men that seemed to led the English game. This would be incorrect for these players were talented as well as physical. The English game just walked to a different beat to those on the continent. If the Dutch game was akin to ballet, them the English game was Hard Rock and there was no doubting how it attracted audiences through its sheer power and physicality. The stadiums became arenas for gladiators and they would rock as triumphs were celebrated. English football – for better or worse – simply stood a step apart from the rest of the world. Even today foreigners will love playing in England for the passion brought to the game by players and supporters. It was unique. Stadiums became cauldrons of emotion, which in turn heightened the hard men being physical, the creative players relishing the adulation as they skipped past a defender. If anything the relationship between the hard men and the supporters was so "bonded" that it made the game that much more physical and intense. It may not have served England well but it made the game exciting and full of athletic prowess and was closer to a Roman amphitheatre than the Ajax team's approach of the early 70s. Of course, this is an exaggerated comment, but one only has to watch the 1970 FA Cup Final – known as The Battle of Wembley – to understand the point.

In the 1970s, and for the 100 years predating, the FA Cup Final was the most glamorous day in the calendar. It was one of the few matches televised and it was a competition that every player wanted to play in and win. In those days, it was often asked whether a player would prefer to win the league or score the winning goal in the Cup

Final. In 1970, the final pitted Revie's Leeds United against the London glamour boys from Chelsea. Both teams boasted players of great skill and flair and players of brute force – and both were seen in both matches (the Final was replayed at Old Trafford with Chelsea defeating Leeds 2–1 after a 2–2 draw at Wembley). If one watches the match carefully, there were not a few off the ball incidents as players took the rules in their own hands. On one occasion, Eddie Gray – the Leeds winger had made Dave Webb (Chelsea central defender) look foolish as he went past him with ease. Ron Harris decided that this could not happen again and so took matters into his own hands with a subtle kick behind the referees back. Today it would be a scandal. In 1970, it was accepted. It was seen to be a man's game and skilful players needed to be able to handle themselves as the hard men came to play.

Recently the match was analysed by today's standards and it was noted that the replay would have seen six red cards and 20 yellow cards.

To supporters of that generation, the memory will bring a wry smile and the game was fun with its mavericks and hard men trading moments of skill, cynicism and sheer brutality. There are literally hundreds of stories circulating of how the hard men took the laws into their hands and they were loved for it.

But it was not an environment to encourage the technical skills that were needed in order to compete on the world stage. And, of course, England didn't. They sat in the wilderness for the decade often wondering and debating why the First Division was viewed to be the best in the world, why the English teams could win the major European Competitions and yet struggle at international level.

In retrospect, it makes one shake one's head as the answer lay so clearly in front of everyone. There was little comparison between the English club game and those in Italy, Germany or Holland. In those countries, the club game was immensely important but the international game was known to be of another level. They had learnt about the importance of physical preparation, diet and rest whilst England's players played more games than anyone else with greater intensity, at greater speed and with more physicality. Even before the players stepped onto the pitch, The England players were at a disadvantage. Their bodies were not as fresh, they were not as physically primed and technically they began to lag behind with each passing year. From 1968 onwards, the Europeans made greater strides in skill, training and preparation and it became a harder and harder task to match.

In Jimmy Case's autobiography, there is a story that strikes a chord about the great Liverpool manager Bob Paisley. Liverpool had lost two matches in a row during the late seventies and suddenly they seemed vulnerable. There was a headline in a newspaper stating the "The Empire is Crumbling". Paisley called the players together for a team meeting and told them:

"We've been watching what you've been eating, trying to find out what's been going bloody wrong. Well, we have found out what's been going wrong, haven't we, Joe, Ronnie (His coaches)?" There was a pause and then Bob continued: "Some of ya have been playing golf," and then he said, "our training schedule can cope with all your beer and your women ... but the bloody golf is out."[56]

It is easy to criticise Revie for his tactics and team selections during his reign but all the signs he displayed were of a man that started with belief and gradually realised the scale of the challenge, lost belief, arguably even became depressed and sought a way out. It is widely accepted that the end of his reign was disappointing and

56   *Hard Case*. Formby Books 2014. The autobiography of Jimmy Case.

that he made an error of judgement. The man has been disgraced and lambasted from every direction but no one has stopped to ask why a good football man, a man that clearly loved English football has made such a decision?

The answer that is often pointed at is money and of course that it how it came across – that Revie became a mercenary, but the truth is probably more complex. Revie had loved building Leeds United. He had wanted to replicate that success with England and the failure to achieve his goal would have hurt him deeply. He had grown up in English football. He had lived and breathed it. He hated how Brian Clough had taken over at Leeds and how he had tried to change what had been successful. The man breathed English football. He only departed as he felt he could succeed. It was not just failure that hurt him; it was the knowledge that he could not find the answer, the truth was that England lagged in technical skill and fitness behind his main European opponents.

Of course, it is simplistic to blame English football for the demise of either Don Revie or George Best. Both were grown men and accountable for their actions but it is fair to say that the pressure of the game played on their insecurities and vulnerabilities. But this is true in any walk of life, which is in the public eye – actors, actresses and politicians have many stories of self-destruction. It does go with the territory of being a professional in the public eye.

However, the players that were and became world-class needed an extraordinary level of self-discipline in order to succeed and stay at the top of their game. Peters, Hurst, Ball, Charlton all possessed this discipline. Moore to a far lesser extent as he enjoyed a drink, he was touched by natural greatness but sadly died at the early age of 53. However, maybe the player that most embodied English football in the 70s was Kevin Keegan.

Kevin Keegan.

By his own admission, Kevin Keegan was not the most naturally talented player but he possessed self-discipline, a great work ethic, determination and a genuine passion to succeed – a passion that was maybe best seen when he was manager of Newcastle United. He inspired a club and city to believe in itself again in the early 90s and how they responded. He took Newcastle from the foot of the second division to the top of the Premier League, challenging Alex Ferguson's Manchester United for the title in 96.

But back in the early 70s, Keegan was a budding talent, recruited by Liverpool from Scunthorpe United. Over the next six years he rose to become England's best player, captain, win the European Cup with Liverpool and become European Footballer of the year for two seasons in a row in 1979 and 1980. Considering Keegan was small in stature and rose up three leagues to Liverpool, it was a genuine rags to riches story but backed up a man with steel and raw determination within him.

He was no one's fool as was evident from the way a small man could compete as a striker against the hard men that have been described in this chapter. He was fast, he developed a great sense for making runs that opened up defences and he could score great goals. He became a Liverpool icon quickly and broke into the England squad in 1972. By 1975, he was already regarded as one of the country's best players. In 1977, as Liverpool competed for the treble of League Championship, FA Cup and European Cup, Keegan announced that he would be leaving for foreign lands after the end of the season. Liverpool was shaken, but his play never let up bar, arguably in the 1977 FA Cup Final against Liverpool's great foes in Manchester United. It was a tense game lost 2–1 and with it the dreams of the treble and Keegan just did not have his best game.

Many muttered that Keegan was not hungry and had his eyes already on his big payday move. But nothing could be further from the truth – it had been just one of those days, as he showed with his display four days later as Liverpool went for the European Cup in the Stadio Olympico in Rome. Keegan ran his German opponents ragged and won the Penalty to seal the triumph as the great German defender, Bert Vogts, could not live with Keegan's pace and direct running and took his legs from underneath him.

Keegan left Liverpool a hero and was one of the biggest names in European football. He could have gone to any of the biggest name clubs but instead choose Hamburg who were hardly one of the top clubs in European football, but Keegan knew where he would thrive and prosper and he did – winning the European Footballer of the Year Crown twice with Hamburg before he again shocked everyone by returning to play for Southampton and not for one for the big name clubs.

Keegan may have made his name under the great Bill Shankly but he was always his own man. It was this trait that made him England's most successful player of his generation. He mixed pace, power, the physical and skill allied with self-discipline and turned himself into a world class player – arguably England's one world-class player from 77–80.

"England danced to a different tune to other countries, but sadly they were dancing ballet whilst we were rock 'n roll and guess what?"

Colin (Supporter).[57]

11.

THE MAVERICK AND THE GENIUS

When one writes about the 70s, it would be wrong not to dedicate a chapter to Brian Clough – a manger that could outrage, alienate and inspire. Whatever one's views of Clough, his achievements were remarkable with small unfashionable clubs. He took Derby County to the League Championship in 1972 and to the semi-finals of the European Cup in 1973, only to lose to the great Juventus side after some dubious refereeing decisions. Later he took Nottingham Forest from mid-table in the Second Division to become League Champions in 1978 and then European Champions in 1979 and 1980. It was truly remarkable as was the man.

It is often stated that Clough was the best manager never to have managed England. Many believe that he should have been appointed as manager in 1978 but Greenwood was a sensible choice after the Revie years. Greenwood steadied the ship and gave England the platform to be competitive once again. Clough would have been a risky and brave choice in 1974 instead of Revie, but arguably would have been the better choice as he was "in tune" with the times and players. He would have been a good choice in 1982 and arguably had a stronger claim that Bobby Robson who had been an excellent manager of Ipswich but had not won as much as Clough. But Clough was seen to be too much his own man, not a "company man".

Clough did walk to a different beat to other managers. What made him stand apart – and arguably the main reason why he should have been given the chance to manage England – was that he understood players, built real bonds of friendship and following and instinctively understood how to influence the psychology of the moment. Clough would never use intimidation to influence; he had his own unique methodology. In fact, he disliked physical foul play, which is why he had such a bitter rivalry with Revie's Leeds. He believed in the passing game and he believed in players playing in the spirit of the game. He was better equipped both psychologically and tactically be a good England manager than Don Revie – but it would have taken a very brave man to have appointed Clough in 1974.

Clough was never just average and certainly never dull. In his playing days, scored 251 league goals from 274 starts playing for Middleborough and Sunderland. He also won two England caps, and was seen as a star of the future but he was forced to retire from playing at the age of 29, after sustaining anterior cruciate ligament damage. Even in his playing days, he showed a different maturity, once stopping the team bus to give an old lady a lift.

In 1965, Clough took the manager's job at Fourth Division Hartlepool United. In 1967 took over at Second Division Derby County. In 1968–69, Derby were promoted as Second Division Champions and just three years later, Derby were crowned League Champions for the first time in the club's history.

In the summer of 1974 he became manager of Leeds United, but was sacked after 44 days in the job. It was arguably the lowest moment in his career. Clough really did believe that the culture at Leeds was wrong and that they did not play the game in the right spirit. He set about change, but rather than achieving it in a softly, softly gradual fashion sought to revolutionise a club that had been run by Don Revie for a long period of time. It raised a fair question over whether Clough could manage star players. Clough's record is remarkable in building teams with unfashionable clubs and in building careers, but could he manage a team of proven internationals?

At Nottingham Forest he built a team of stars, but he built the team. The question was could he inherit a team of stars and win them over. There is a difference and those that argue that he should never have been in the frame to manage England point to this. It is a fair argument but he managed no few great players over the years. The truth is more likely to lie with Clough wanting to make an instant impact and letting his beliefs cloud his judgement.

Clough had resigned from Derby in 73 and had taken over at Brighton for a short eight month period. It was not a particularly successful time and the offer of the role with Leeds was Clough's return to the top of league management and with a club that he genuinely believed had issues to resolve. Leeds United under Revie had been the country's leading team and there is little doubt that they did intimidate. They had great passing players with great skill, but they could also resort to the cynical as the occasion dictated. Clough was a purist to Revie's pragmatist and the two developed a genuine dislike for each other. It was also known that Revie had wanted Johnny Giles – one of his players – to take over; so the background was already charged before day one and it would take any manager skill to win the team over. The players were concerned about Clough's appointment and they never connected to the man. It was a situation that happens in all walks of life when the cultural fit between a manager and the environment is out of sync. Clough made clear mistakes but history will show that most struggle to take over from an established figurehead in any walk of life whether football, politics or business.

Within months Clough bounced back joining Second Division Nottingham Forest, and so began a remarkable journey. When Forest won the Championship in 1978, Clough became one of only four managers to have won the English league with two different clubs.

Forest also won two consecutive European Cups (in 1979 and 1980) and two League Cups (1978 and 1979).

If one compares Clough to Bobby Robson's achievements – Robson won the FA Cup in 1976 and the UEFA Cup in 1981 – then Clough had stronger credentials although Robson had played more international football. In time, Robson proved himself to be one of the greatest managers of his generation and he was a successful England manager, building one of England's best ever teams.

However, all the above only tells part of the story about Brian Clough. The man was unique and built a special bond with players. Those that had that bond would swear by the man and have run through brick walls. There were others that kept apart from the man. If one reads all the many stories that circulate about Clough, his success did come from two core skills – firstly, his use of psychology to make players feel relaxed and to enjoy a challenge and secondly, he was a fatherly paternal figure to his players, but then so were all the great managers of that era – Shankly, Paisley, and Revie. The question was how he could bring the best out of his players.

It is worth highlighting a number of stories about the man that bring a smile to the face. Some of the following may be legends, but have a basis in truth:[58]

-   David Hay was manager of Celtic when they played Nottingham Forest in European Competition. Celtic had drawn 1–1 at the City Ground and were confident of achieving success at Celtic Park. A day before the match in Glasgow, Hay was training with his players when he received a call from a contact who told him not only had Nottingham Forest arrived in Glasgow, but that Clough had taken the team to David Hay's own pub near the airport and that they were mingling with

---

locals, enjoying a pint. It was a typical Clough move, as in one move he had relaxed the players by getting them to mix and banter with the locals in David Hay's – the opposition manager – own pub. It was a masterstroke and Forest won the match 2–1.

-   Clough was once asked how he managed a player who would dispute a decision. He is reputed to have replied, "I would sit then down with a cup of tea, we would discuss the issue for twenty minutes and then we would agree I was right."

-   In 1978, Forest were travelling to Wembley to play the League Cup Final against Liverpool. Forest had a still inexperienced team and Liverpool were the Champions of England and Europe, Clough stopped the team bus at a pub, enjoyed a pint with the players before returning to their journey. The Players were relaxed and drew the match 0–0.

-   Once he helped pick an all star international team and when asked who should manager the team, he responded: "Well it'd have to be someone who's played a bit, could talk about it clearly without waffling on as if he was Albert Einstein, some-one who wouldn't be afraid to tell that Cruyff bloke to pass the ball. I suppose it had better be me!"

-   The Journalist Pat Murphy once spoke about Clough's mana-gerial style:[59] "I often used to think the Forest side of the 1980s was too relaxed at the start of a match. The players would run onto the pitch, seemingly without a care in the world.

---

59   http://www.bbc.co.uk/sport/0/football/29145641 [Accessed: Sept 2014].

That was because a Clough team-talk would rarely last a minute – no hairdryers, no ranting. He would place a ball on the physio's couch and say: "That's your best friend for the next couple of hours. Treat it like your wife or girlfriend – caress it, love it. This after making his players listen to Frank Sinatra, Matt Monro or the Ink Spots. The thoughts of that great punk fan, current Forest boss Stuart Pearce, were never sought by his manager. "I had enough of tedious team talks when I was a player," Clough once told me. "Footballers don't have a long attention span; they are instinctive."

He would get irritated at the idea of micro-managing footballers and demanded that they relaxed once they knew what was necessary. "Come and see my coaching certificates – they're called the European Cup and League Championships," he once said.

- One of his players once commented "If I had a great match, he would then admit that to journalists. He would say that I had played alright. If, though, I had played really badly, he would have told the journalists I was the best player on the field. That was the man – he would be there for you on the bad days but never let you get big headed"

- Martin O'Neill once commented that: "It was one of the great myths that he was a manager, not a coach," O'Neill said. "Every day was a coaching lesson from Brian Clough. You'd pick up something that would last you a lifetime."[60]

60   http://www.dailymail.co.uk/sport/football/article-2181529/Martin-ONeill-delves-Brian-Clough-memories-bid-lift-Sunderland.html [Accessed: September 2014].

- Justin Fashanu had been signed for Forest from Norwich City and Fashanu – a shy man – had struggled to settle and play well. Clough suggested that Fashanu rejoin Norwich. One day Fashanu, a deeply religious man, came to Clough's office and told him that he had spoken to God and God had told him not to return to Norwich. Clough is reputed to have replied, "Son, there is only one God in Nottingham and he tells you to go to Norwich."

- "I wouldn't say I was the best manager in the business but I was in the top one."

- Don't send me flowers when I'm dead. If you like me, send them while I'm alive."

- "If God had wanted us to play football in the clouds, he'd have put grass up there."

Some of the above may have been tweaked as stories with time but there is little doubt that Clough was a unique man. One can debate for hours whether or not Clough should have been appointed England manager over Revie, Greenwood or Robson but the under-lying point is that England possessed a number of great managers from which to choose. One could add in Dave Sexton (Chelsea), Malcolm Allison (Man City), and Bill Nicholson (Spurs) – all who had achieved success in European Competition. Nicholson had won the double for Spurs in 1961 and built two great Spurs teams.

Just as England possessed great players, so it had the managers to match. However, in the 1970s, the managers were feudal lords of their Kingdoms. They were dominant characters who were father figures to the players. They were masters on their clubs and this freedom did allow characters such as Clough to flourish. They could be autocratic and strong, outspoken figures. The game and the club environment allowed that to happen.

Again, though, international football was a different discipline and required a different skill. The managers had only limited time with the players and could not be the "strong leadership" figures that could be at their clubs. The English game just did not prepare the ground for the international arena. When Bobby Robson did take over in 1982, he failed to qualify for his first international competition and stated that it did take two years to adapt to the international stage after club football.

One could argue that a Walter Winterbottom type character was best suited to the role and if the 1958 Munich tragedy had not ripped greater players from the England team, it may have been that Winterbottom would have been far better remembered. But such is life. The role could also have been suited to proven managers at the end of their careers who were looking for a different challenge – managers such as Bill Nicholson or, of course, Ron Greenwood.

Greenwood had built the great West Ham team of Moore, Peters and Hurst. He had won the FA Cup and the European Cup Winners' Cup. He made the club known as "The Academy of Football" and respected across the country. He had handed over the reigns as manager to John Lyall and had moved into a senior administration role. As Revie resigned, the FA turned to the proven, experience of Greenwood to build a recovery. Just maybe the FA made the right decision as they called for Greenwood.

"I remember the arguments in my house between my brother and father over systems. Everything was about the defensive. My father would go on about Stanley Mattthews and Tom Finney. I am sure they were great playersbut it was all such rubbish. Football was simply get more technically evolved and for some weird reason, the English just ignored it. We were arrogant for years until defeat after defeat made us a little bit more humble. We would believe that English football was still the best in the world even though we could never qualify for international tournaments. Being good was about winning when it mattered. The English believed their own PR."

Donald[61]

12.

'GIVE US SOMETHING TO CHEER'
THE RISE OF A NEW GENERATION

One of the greatest aspects of English football is that is anything but predictable. In the 1970s, it was a bit like a wild animal, not quite in control. The turbulent period of hooliganism began and it was like watching rival tribes bait each other at times. But the bond between the footballers and the players was very strong and the game was still about the fans on the terraces, singing their songs, chanting to their players who were heroes within their tribes and communities. It is a bond that has been lost in the modern game but in the 1970s, the emotion within the stadiums and the bond between player and supporters was intense and fiercely loyal.

It is a strange contradiction that does make the English game stand both tall and alone. The intensity within grounds was something to behold. The players that enjoyed playing in electric atmospheres would feel those few feet taller and raise their games. One can look at pictures of Martin Peters from the 70s and one will see a slim, almost slight figure that does not appear as though he would have been one of the leading figures of this story. But watch him live, in those days, and he exuded a confidence and charisma that has been lost in the pictures that tell the story of the time. Many would marvel at the passion that filled English stadiums but at the same time, the game was so caught up in its own arrogance and belief, it hindered the English clubs learning from abroad and developing. The British have always possessed an "islander" mentality – sometimes for the better as in the Second World War and sometimes for the worse, as in the 70s. The game believed it was the best league in the world. We believed that we still possessed some of the game's greatest players; that if the manager could get the selection right that England would once again sit at the top table in international football. The idea of changing diets, physical preparation and coaching did fall on deaf ears. The English club was thriving and stars were being created.

For a period of time, the game did seem though to entering a dark period as hooliganism began to cross the boundary of social acceptability just at a time when England needed support. At the same time, the players were increasingly becoming more than the working class heroes of old, but superstars with the ability to make fortunes. Arguably, Kevin Keegan was the first of England's superstar players as a new age was ushered in.

But the new age was not all bad. Just as it seemed that defensive systems had the upper hand over the flair players in the early 70s, so suddenly rose a new generation of highly talented players that lay the foundations for England's return from exile. Just as the seeds for success for England's 1966 triumph began in the 1950s, so the roots of England's 1990 team began in the mid 70s with the rise of a whole array for talent led by Trevor Francis and Ray Wilkins, and followed by the emergence of Glen Hoddle, Laurie Cunningham, Kenny Sansom, Bryan Robson, Terry Butcher, Steve Coppell, Peter Barnes, Cyrile Regis, Tony Woodcock, and Graham Rix. These players changed the landscape of English football as they were not one-club players but were ambitious, skilful and had their eyes of an exciting future. Over the next fifteen years, Trevor Francis and Ray Wilkins would play for top Italian teams; Glen Hoddle for Monaco: Laurie Cunningham for Real Madrid; and Tony Woodcock for FC Cologne. Suddenly the game had strength in depth again and one could see that England would become a force again.

All the above players played major roles but the ones that really did evolve the English game arguably were Francis, Wilkins, Hoddle and Cunningham. These four in very different ways excited audiences and led the change in fortunes.

Ray "Butch" Wilkins.

It is strange to write about the young Ray Wilkins as in the mid 70s, he was seen as a natural successor to Bobby Moore, as a charismatic future England Captain. He made his debut in 1973 at the age of 17, excited observers with his potential and became Captain of Chelsea at the age of 18 succeeding the great Ron Harris. Wilkins was soon a pin up boy of the industry. Fast forward seven or eight years and Wilkins had begun to develop a reputation as a negative player who would always pass sideways and was the foil to the dynamic Bryan Robson. At the end of the day, Wilkins won 84 caps for England and played for Chelsea, Manchester United, AC Milan, Paris St. Germain, Rangers and QPR. If one had outlined such a career to the young 17-year-old as he made his debut, he would have been very happy and yet one always feels that Wilkins never fulfilled his potential. Ask most of their memories of Wilkins and they will remember the great goal he scored in the FA Cup Final in 1983, or his sending off against Morocco in the World Cup of 1986 or his side passing – when he was nicknamed "The Crab" by his own manager.

But the counter to this perception and part of the story that has been lost with time is that Wilkins did lead the way for the young generation that would become England's star of the 1980s.

Wilkins must have been a special talent, a special leader, for Chelsea to make him captain at the age of 18 to follow Ron Harris. Admittedly, the manager – Eddie McCreadie – was building a new young side following relegation in the 1974–75 season which won promotion back to the First Division in the 1976–77 season play-ing some exceptionally exciting football. Wilkins made his England debut in 1976 in New York as Revie's England defeated Italy 3–2. However, following McCreadie resignation as manager and Chelsea struggled and were relegated in 1978–79 season. A short while later, Wilkins was transferred to Manchester United for £800,000 which was a significant fee for the time. Wilkins enjoyed five seasons with United, but he appeared to change as a player and lost some of the inspiration that was so evident as he kicked off his career. He played his last match for England in 1986.

Wilkins will always be a paradox to many football fans. He was an inspiration in his early days that never fully realised his talent but did score, on occasions, crucial goals in the big matches, such as the Cup Final goal against Brighton or England's opening goal versus Belgium in the 1980 European Championships. He could score great goals too such as for Chelsea versus Hereford United in 1976–77 season when he chipped the goalkeeper from outside the box with great vision, or for Rangers in the derby match versus Celtic.

It is clear that Wilkins is a genuine, good football man and has enjoyed a good career in coaching but he has always seemed to be a better number two than number one – and there lies the question – what happened to the inspirational young leader that took the stage in 1973. Why and when did he change from being the leader to being the excellent foil/number two that he was for Robson with Man Utd and England and even at Rangers between 1987–89.

The answer does not matter; Wilkins made a phenomenal contri-bution and helped lead England back to competitiveness.

Trevor Francis

Francis will always be known as the first £1m footballer when Nottingham Forest acquired him from Birmingham City in 1979. He went on the score Forest's winning goal in the 1979 European Cup Final versus Malmo, that was such an important part of the Brian Clough story of taking Forest from the Second Division to Champions of Europe.

Francis, in the mid 70s, was England's most exciting young forward – best symbolised by the goal he scored in 1976 against QPR when he beat four players on his way to score. He made his England debut for England in 1977 in the 2–0 loss to Holland. At the time, Birmingham were a mid-table team that achieved little in terms of honours, but in Francis had a player that excited crowds with a display of skills that made him seem like a mini replica of Johnan Cruyff.

After Birmingham, it always seemed that Francis struggled to settle. He played for Birmingham form 1971–79, then for Forest from 1979–1981; Manchester City from 1981–82. Like Wilkins, Francis did appear to be a player that never quite fulfilled his potential, although he did enjoy a successful four years with Sampdoria (1982–86), which he clearly enjoyed and flourish with. But after, he spent one season with Atalanta and one with Rangers. Francis played 52 times for England, scoring 12 goals.

One always wonders if he had stayed at Birmingham and if Birmingham could have had a stronger set-up, what could Francis have achieved?

Peter Barnes

The story of Peter Barnes is a good reflection of the period as he possessed so much potential and more importantly, Barnes played a pivotal role on England's left wing in the revival under Greenwood. He made his debut in 1977 against Italy at Wembley and played his last game, after 22 caps, in 1982 – aged 25. Barnes had shown in the 1977–78 season that he had the skill and aptitude for the international game, but was it and he really nurtured as best as could be? Could Barnes have provided the missing inspiration in the second stages of the 82 World Cup as England tried to find a way though the West German and Spanish defences?

Barnes started his career with much promise. He scored in Manchester City's League Cup victory over Newcastle in 1976. He was also named PFA Young Player of the Year and then made his England debut in 1977. It seemed as though the game was easy. He made such a thrilling start to internationals, as they did scare the Italian defence at Wembley. He became a regular in the team, scored the equaliser in the 3–1 victor over Scotland at Wembley, played in five of the qualifying matches for Euro 80, scoring against Bulgaria (away) but then was not taken to the Finals in Italy. It is hard to fully understand as the potential was there for all to see and especially as his goal scoring record at international level was one in four.

In 1979, he was bought by WBA (Ron Atkinson) for a club record fee of £748,000 and Atkinson would sign him again when manager for Manchester United. Barnes is one of a very few players that played for both Manchester clubs.

Barnes loved his football and became a footballing globe-trotter as he played for an estimated 30 clubs over his career.

Was Barnes another that England should have nurtured better?

Laurie Cunningham

Few recall Laurie Cunningham as either Wilkins or Francis are recalled but back in 1979, Laurie Cunningham was bought by the great Real Madrid from West Brom. Cunningham should have been one of England's great first black players that played many times with Wilkins and Francis on England's return but that story was not to unfold.

He joined West Bromwich Albion in 1977, but it was under Ron Atkinson that Cunningham came to the fore as one of the "Three Degrees" as he teamed up with, Cyrille Regis, and Brendon Batson. Arguably this was one of West Brom's most exciting teams of the last 40 years. They certainly became one of the most attractive and exciting English sides in the late 1970s. It was only a matter of time before Cunningham would come to the fore, as he was the star player.

He became the second black player to wear an England shirt at any level in the England under-21s' friendly against Scotland at Bramall Lane on 27 April 1977, scoring on his debut. He made his full England debut against Wales in a Home International in 1979 and went on to win a total of six caps for England.

In the summer of 1979, he made a historic move as the first British player to transfer to Real Madrid, who paid West Bromwich Albion a fee of £950,000. He scored twice on his debut and helped Real win the league and cup double. Despite this club success, Cunningham was overlooked by England manager Ron Greenwood for a place in the England squad for Euro 1980. Cunningham continued his success with Real Madrid and played – against Liverpool – in the 1981 European Cup Final. He made his last England appearance in 1982 against Romania.

One has to wonder what Cunningham could have achieved with England if he had been given time and more opportunity? One can argue that larger clubs seemed to hinder both Wilkins and Francis's development and yet Cunningham seemed to play his best football for Real Madrid. Maybe the international stage may have brought the best out of the player?

It will, of course, be one of life's great unanswered questions and he has never been able to really explain his thoughts and perspective in retrospect as sadly Cunningham died in a car crash in 1989 at the young age of 33.

Glenn Hoddle

Much has been written about Glenn Hoddle and it is well known that he was one of the most skilful players of his time. He seemed to play a different game to other England players with his subtle touches and wide range of passing. Even in a Tottenham midfield that included World Cup winning players such as Ossie Ardiles and Ricky Villa, Hoddle stood up and was a leader. In the early 80s, Spurs played some the best football since the 60s as they genuinely challenged for the league title – inspired by the midfield axis of Hoddle and Ardiles. Hoddle made the game look easy and appeared to have so much time on the ball. Many managers admired the players but struggled to build teams around him. It was the Spurs manager, Keith Burkinshaw that really brought out the best of the player as both a player and a midfield general.

It can be argued that Tottenham's relegation after the 1976–77 season helped Hoddle emerge as a player as he became the "Star" player" as Spurs won promotion after one season. Hoddle's skill and vision made Spurs stand a step above.

He made his England debut in November 1979 and scored a goal in a 2–0 win that had expert commentators purring in delight. He followed this up with four goals in his first 10 Internationals, but he struggled ever to become a regular in the England midfield until after the 1982 World Cup. He played only 53 times for England over nine years and only achieved regular selection under Bobby Robson for the 86 World Cup and 88 European Championships. Greenwood's preference was for the solidity of Wilkins, Coppell, Robson and Rix in midfield for the 1982 finals and England came home undefeated but they did not win either of the second stage matches against West Germany (0–0) and Spain (0–0). Brooking was Greenwood's creative midfield player but he was injured for the majority of the 82 finals. One has to wonder if Hoddle's creativity could have unlocked the German or Spanish defences in those crucial stages. He played only as a substitute in the opening stage group matches against Kuwait and Czechoslovakia.

In fairness, Hoddle never was able to assert himself on the international stage as he could with Spurs. The Spurs team was built around him and he flourished. With England, he was just another player and the England managers could not just build a team around one player, as they needed more in their armoury.

Even when he was a regular, he rarely dominated matches at international level. His most striking performances where when he was a young player breaking through and in the latter years, it was almost as he felt hindered to play with the freedom he needed. Against Argentine in 86, he is best remembered for being one of the players Maradona ran past for his wonder goal and his last appearance was for a broken team against the Soviet Union in the 1988 European Championships.

Hoddle became England manager in succession to Terry Venables in 1996 and could have become a great international manager. He evolved and built a very good team that played in the one of the best matches of the 1998 World Cup in France against Argentine – the match that made Michael Owen's name as an international striker as he ran at the Argentinian defence to score a wonderful solo goal. The game ended 2–2 and England lost on penalties, but the team had played most of the second half with 10 men after David Beckham's sending off.

Hoddle sadly lost the job after some controversial personal comments came to light but he was a man that really did understand the game at the highest level. Bar those comments, he could have had a better career as manager than as a player, which is a thought-provoking observation for one of England's finest creative midfielders.

Bryan Robson

Just as it was difficult to fit Hoddle into the England structure and system, so Robson was every manager's dream with his fearless tackling, great running, stamina and goalscoring ability. Robson was a natural leader that seemed to inspire England on during the mid 90s almost on his own.

Robson first came to notice as one of the players that won the "mini" World Cup in 1975. At the time, many administrators used this to point to future England prosperity through the strength of its young players. Robson made his league debut for West Bromwich Albion in 1975 but only really broke into the team in 1976. He made his England debut in 1980 and in 1981, made a record transfer to Manchester United for 1.5 million. Over the next decade, Robson won 90 caps and scored 26 goals including one of the fastest in World Cup history against France at the start of the 82 finals – timed at 27 seconds.

For England the combination of Robson under Bobby Robson's management made a strong united team of manager and captain. Both were from the North East. Both were passionate about England

and both were resolute under pressure, which certainly followed the 1988 England performances in the European Championships in West Germany.

Robson was nicknamed "Captain Marvel" and highly rated by the players and managers with whom he played. However, it is only fair to note that England performed better after Robson was injured in both the 1986 World Cup and 1990 World Cup. There is little doubt that Robson was a great player – almost archetypal in the English way – but was he the best leader for the international arena? Did his approach hinder more creative players from playing with the freedom they needed? Or – what may be a fairer question – did Robson's presence stop other players taking on accountability, as they should?

Whatever the truth of the matter, England did play better football after his injuries in 86 which brought Peter Reid, the Everton Midfield general, into the team and in 1990 which kick started David Platt's international career.

The mid 70s saw the rise of a new generation of players that did come together to work for England's cause, as he did rise back to a position of credibility. Whether the players achieved all they could is open to debate, but in the overall scheme of things it is unimportant. Some players overachieve; some underachieve. They all reached and played at the highest levels of the game and became star names of the era.

The FA CUP Final – The 1970s

If one wants to view how the game changed during the 1970s, one only needs to look at the FA Cup Finals that took place during that decade. The FA Cup Final was the most prestigious and glamorous day of the season. Every player wanted to be part of the occasion and every fan wanted to see their team hoist the cup above their heads in triumph. The game was broadcast live all across the globe and was of major importance.

The decade began with the couple of matches that did fully illustrate the competitive and brutal nature of the game. Chelsea and Leeds United came together to play the Final and drew the match at Wembley 2–2. In the views of many, Leeds were the better team and it was an individual error by the Leeds goalkeeper, Gary Sprake that let Chelsea grew in confidence. The replay at Old Trafford though was as tough an encounter as seen in the history of FA Cup Finals. The replay was recently analysed against modern standards and David Elleray – an experienced referee in the modern game – noted that six players would have had red cards and that twenty yellow cards would have been shown. In the modern day, the game would have been seen as a scandal but in 1970, it was passed off as being played in a competitive spirit. Chelsea won the replay 2–1.

Arsenal won the 1971 final to win the double. The Arsenal team of 71 was reflective of the era – strong in defence, a real team with few star players. The forward line of Charlie George, Ray Kennedy and John Radford boasted two young exciting talents with a solid strong centre-forward. The team was built on a strong defence led by Frank McLintock that would give little away, but in the 71 season the team were motivated, inspired and played beyond the sum of all their parts. Very few teams that have won the double could have possessed so few genuinely regular international players. It was a classic example of the system combined with a fine blend of experience and youth finding their purple moment.

However the real story of the 1970s finals lay in how teams from the second tier of the competition were able to regularly reach the Final and be competitive. The 1970s was the era where good Second Division teams were able to compete almost on an equal basis with their superior First Divisions teams over a short period of time. In

1973, Sunderland shocked the nation by beating Leeds United 1–0. Fulham – with Bobby Moore and Alan Mullery in their ranks for their final big match – played West Ham in the 1975 Final, only to lose 2–0. Southampton won the 1976 Final (1–0) against the rising, exciting team of Manchester United under Tommy Docherty and West Ham won the 1980 Final (1–0) over their London rivals, Arsenal.

All these Second Division teams possessed a mix of great organization coupled with a number of excellent, experienced players that could mix with the best.

- Sunderland had in their ranks Dave Watson (who would become England's centre half for a number of years), Jim Montgomery and Ian Porterfield.

- Fulham had Moore and Mullery.

- Southampton boasted even more quality in Mick Channon, Peter Osgood and Jim McCalliog.

- West Ham had Trevor Brooking, Phil Parkes, Stuart Pearson, Frank Lampard and Billy Bonds.

Some will argue that it showed the strength in depth of the league teams in the First and Second divisions. True. It also showed how close the two divisions had become and how a well-organised team could compete to a level.

"I know that the stadiums today are much safer and family friendly but I do really miss the tension and violent edge of the 70s. I know I should not admit to it but games today do lack that extra edge".

Andy.[62]

13.

THE RISE OF THE FALLEN.

If you looks back at international football in the 1970s, it is clear that England simply neither evolved their thinking from the success under Ramsey nor did they heed the lessons of what was taking place on the international scene.

Ramsey achieved success through creating a winning formula that combined a number of great players within a system that played to their strengths. Ramsey's system brought the best out of Bobby Charlton who could run at sides from midfield and make them defensive in their mind-set with his threat. Peters could "ghost" into positions to score goals. Ball added energy and guile whilst Banks and Moore were simply giants in their positions, able to repel attackers. But Ramsey's success did rely on great organization and the core of great players. Once this core broke down – as was seen against West Germany in both 1970 and in 1972 – then England were vulnerable. England believed that they had one of the best teams in the world but the truth was that it relied on a few great players. This lasted till 1970 but after the Mexico World Cup, the players began to fade and England's troubles began.

Of course, there was more depth to the problems that were to come. England still possessed a range of potentially exceptional players waiting in the wings to learn how to play at the highest level. Ramsey though continued with his tried and tested formula whilst other teams evolved their approach, thinking and technical play to break down well organised sides. The English club teams of the early 1970s all followed Ramsey's lead and the leading teams were all well organised, compact and very competitive. The game for the early years of the 1970s did not encourage players with skill and flair that wanted to be attack minded. Defence was the foundations stones on which winning teams were built.

However, Brazil had won the World Cup in 1970 with thrilling play that made the game appear beautiful. Yes England competed effectively with Brazil and they could – and maybe should have drawn 1–1. However, that would have been a successful result for England whilst Brazil could have beaten England 2–0. Brazil respected England and played the game accordingly. Against other sides, their attacking play inspired children all across the world to play the game with panache. Already teams were working out that a well-organised team was vulnerable against excellent ball players that could do the inspired. Brazil led the way and this was followed by both Holland and West Germany in 1974. Both teams were well organised and had attacking philosophies.

If one can sit back objectively and imagine how the England team that played Poland in 1973 would have fared against the Holland side of Cruyff and Neeskens, then in truth England was still a step behind. Ramsey's fresh new team of 73 could have grown into an excellent international team with Tony Currie, Martin Chivers, Colin Bell, Peter Shilton and Roy McFarland as its core, but they were simply not ready for the immediate challenge. Ramsey maybe realised too late that the game had evolved and he needed to change. In fairness to the great man, he did change and he was building a new team, but it was just a year too late. Given another year and England could have fielded a team that were quarter-finalists. England had the calibre of player and quality to compete to a good level in 74 and in 78 but the English obsession with defence and systems underplayed the need for developing international flair players that could unlock defences.

Make no mistake; England possessed the depth and quality of player that could have been developed into very good international players, but for many reasons never quite made it beyond a certain level. Think of Tony Currie, Martin Chivers, Gerry Francis, Colin Todd, Roy McFarland, David Nish, Alan Hudson, Allan Clarke, Ray Kennedy, Keith Weller, Frank Worthington, Billy Bonds, Graham Paddon and Jimmy Case.

Joe Mercer, in his short period of time, managed to find a balance between defence and attacking flair that had England playing competitive football again. It arguably needed a man that was one step removed from club football and maybe Mercer would have the right man to succeed Ramsey as he appeared to understand what was needed and more importantly, understood players. He had the ability to bring them together as a united team in a short period of time. Revie never won over the players. Mercer did.

Enter Ron Greenwood who was from the same school of thought as was Mercer and it was to be Greenwood that would be gradually nurse England back to health through finding a balance that encouraged attacking play that could unlock the best defences in the world game.

Historically England's attacking prowess lay in a combination of a strong physical centre-forward combined with wingers that would attack the full-backs and send in cross after cross to threaten the opposition's goal. Ramsey built a system – the wingless wonders – that worked for a period of time until superior teams developed strategies to reduce the threat. In 1977, Greenwood reintroduced an attack minded 4-4-2 with wingers in Peter Barnes and Steve Coppell to great effect. During the late 60s and early 70s, the system had become too important and at international level a team needs the unpredictable to unlock defences. England had become too predictable and their play lacked inspiration and flair. Greenwood's team possessed a balance that has the physical presence of a strong centre-forward – Bob Latchford – served by two wingers and supported with the subtle runs and skill of Trevor Brooking and Kevin Keegan who were the fulcrum of the team. Suddenly England looked balanced and possessed more variety to their play.

If one analyses what are arguably England's two best teams since 1970 in 1990 and 96, one can see the skill and balance to both attack and defend. In 1996, under Terry Venables, England had again the strong physical presence of a traditional English centre-forward in Alan Shearer supported alongside him by the subtle approach play of Terry Sheringham and supported by Steve McManaman and Darren Anderton – both with the ability to unlock a defensive system with a moment of skill – supported by Paul Gascoigne. In defence, England were resolute with David Seaman (Goalkeeper), Tony Adams, Stuart Pearce, Gary Neville, Gareth Southgate and Paul Ince in a holding position. Arguably this was England's most exciting and balanced team since the great days as World Champions and England played some superb football – most especially against Holland who England destroyed 4–1 in the 1996 European Championships.

The 1990 team, under Bobby Robson, also possessed a similar structure with the able Gary Lineker supported by Peter Beardsley and supported by two more excellent wingers in John Barnes and Chris Waddle, Paul Gascoigne played some of his best football as the attacking threat from midfield and David Platt came into the team to score some very important goals with late runs into the box. Again, this line up possessed both balance and the unpredictable skill that could unlock the very best defences. In the rearguard, stood a defence that included Shilton, Terry Butcher, Stuart Pearce, and Paul Parker.

It is easy to see why both these England teams had their golden moments when the team came together as a genuinely competitive force. It also serves to highlight the lack of creativity and flair that existed within the systems that so dominated the 70s. England simply defeated themselves by employing tactics and strategies that had become out-dated. The world game had moved on and England had fallen behind.

The other observation to make is that both the 1996 European Championship team and the 1990 World Cup team seemed to enjoy playing the game under their managers. Once both teams found their feet after nervous starts, both teams played with a fluidity and inspiration that the balance of the team allowed. In Sport, confidence and mind-set is so important and England have always appeared to struggle with the easy confidence of a great team. In 1990, confidence came after the 0–0 draw with Holland in which Gascoigne truly scared the Dutch with his runs at their heart. After the game, England knew they could compete and confidence grew. In 1996, England struggled in the match with Scotland but a moment of brilliance from Paul Gascoigne lifted spirits, won the game and gave the team the confidence to attack the Dutch in their next match.

Football has never been rocket science and has always required successful teams to possess a real craft mix, the balance of attacking prowess and steel in defence and the confidence to really play the game. The 1966 team needed the presence of Jack Charlton and Nobby Stiles to give the freedom to their world-class trio of Charlton, Moore and Peters to play their games. The 1996 team needed the craft of Anderton and McManaman with the steel of Adams and Ince. The 1966, 1996 and 1990 teams all started their tournaments nervously but built confidence through a balance that really threatened the opposition. The 1973 team lacked confidence and the Polish knew they could threaten England. They may have been the underdogs but they knew that they stood a good chance rather than feeling – as they should have – intimidated as they entered the home of England.

History has never been any different. All the great teams – bar 66 – possessed great wing play combined with the steely defence. Consider Stanley Matthews with Tom Finney in the 40s and early 50s. Barnes and Waddle. Barnes and Coppell. Anderton and McManaman.

Greenwood began his reign as England manager in cautious style by trying to bring together the best of England's two most dominant teams in Liverpool and Ipswich. The logic was to try and bring together club combinations that worked effectively week in, week out. But England appeared to lack a real cutting edge. They drew the first match of Greenwood's reign at home 0–0 with Switzerland and then only won 2–0 away to Luxemburg.

For the return match of the 78 World Cup qualifying group against Italy, Greenwood changed his approach and launched a team that excited England's fans in a way that that had not felt since the first year of Revie's reign. Greenwood played a 4-4-2 formation that could move into a 4-2-4 as England attacked and employed the two wings in the young 20-year-old Peter Barnes and Steve Coppell. The Italians appeared a different team to the one that had beaten England with ease in Rome as England attacked from different sides. Kevin Keegan scored early in the match to help build a momentum and Brooking added a second in the second half to complete an encouraging 2–0 victory but it only told half the story. The match saw Barnes attack from the left and make an exciting run that left a couple of Italians in his wake. Latchford was a constant threat as the Italians tried to find stability. It may not have been enough to recover the lost ground but there were encouraging signs and morale was lifted. An attendance of 92,000 cheered a new approach and team.

The real test of Greenwood's rebuilding would come in the next two matches as they would be against the World Champions, West Germany, in Munich (February 1978) and then Brazil at Wembley (April 78). Against the West Germans, England started brightly and scored first through Stuart Pearson but lost momentum as the Germans regained control and won 2–1. Against Brazil, Brazil scored first but England fought back and built real pressure on the Brazilian goal before equalizing through Keegan. Both matches showed that England may have not won, may still have a long way to go but were, at last, on the right tracks.

England completed the season with an encouraging won over their oldest rival, Scotland in Glasgow, which was supposed to provide the Scots with a morale-boosting win before they set sail for Argentina. The Scots had high hopes for their team to perform well in the 1978 finals but the England match was a forerunner of the problems they would encounter in the tournament when they lost their opening match to Peru and then drew with Iran before finally coming together in a famous win over Holland. It was so reminiscent of how English hopes had soared over the past five years but fallen away as they struggled to test either the Peruvian or Iranian defences. It required the Scots to be under huge pressure and some individual brilliance for the Scots to finally show their potential but it was too late.

England began the following season with an exciting 4–3 win over Denmark in Copenhagen – with goals from Keegan (2), Latchford and Neal – to open their European campaign. The 1979 season was to show some exciting, free flowing football, as England were playing with a different tempo. In February 79, England easily defeated Northern Ireland 4–0 at Wembley. They beat Scotland 3–1 at Wembley with some great interchange play between Keegan and Brooking to unlock the Scots for the third goal. England followed this with a summer tour which saw them beat Bulgaria 3–0 in Sofia, then draw 0–0 with Sweden in Stockholm before losing a thrilling match in Vienna, 4–3 to Austria.

England played the 1979 season with width and adventure and it suddenly seemed a long way from the dark days of 1976 and 77. England continued in their adventurous style at the start of the following season with a 1–0 win over Denmark at Wembley, followed by a 5–1 victory over Northern Ireland and a 2–0 win over Bulgaria in a game that heralded the debut of Glenn Hoddle.

With the arrival of 1980, England could look forward to their first international finals since 1970 with the European Championships in Italy. England continued their impressive build up with a 2–0 win in Spain and a 3–1 win over the World Champions, Argentina, at Wembley. All appeared to be rosy but Greenwood had made a subtle change in approach in early 1980 with the dropping of Peter Barnes, who had played an influential role in England's arrival and had provided the extra balance on the left wing to balance Coppell on the right. Against Spain, England played a 4-3-1-2 formation with a forward combination of Francis, Woodcock and Keegan supported by a midfield of Wilkins, Coppell and Ray Kennedy. Keegan played just behind Francis and Woodcock and it was an innovative approach as neither were centre-forwards but two mobile, skilful inside-forwards and it worked very effectively.

Against Argentina, England again lined up in the same formation but with David Johnson starting in place of Trevor Francis. Johnson was a traditional centre-forward, very different in style to the innovative Francis and, although they won the match against

Argentina, England's had lost the balance that had served them so well during the last two years. It was still a bold approach with a team that boasted five forward players in Woodcock, Johnson, Keegan, Coppell and Ray Kennedy – although Kennedy had reverted to being a midfield player. Greenwood never lacked boldness or courage but was the balance to the team as good as it had been over the last 24 months.

In the first match of the European Championships, England played Belgium with 10 of the 11 that had started against Argentina. The one change was to bring Brooking in for Kennedy. Brooking was the more skilful technical player but Kennedy did carry more threat. England started well and Wilkins scored a memorable goal but Belgium came back strongly and arguably were the better team by the end of the match. The next match for England was against their hosts, Italy and it was always going to be a tough match. In the build up to the match, England seemed to lack certainty and it showed in the selection of an inexperienced Gary Birtles (Nottingham Forest) as the lead of England's attack. Birtles had enjoyed an excellent season with Forest but he had literally made his debut as a substitute in the win over Argentina. Was he really a player that had enough in his firepower to trouble the Italians? Greenwood tinkered with the side again replacing Brooking with Kennedy in a 4-3-1-2 formation. The logic was that the Nottingham Forest duo of Woodcock and Birtles could unsettle the Italians but the reality was that Italy won the match with more ease than the 1–0 score line suggested. England played well but the Italians were superior and when the goal came in the 78th minute, it had been expected. England may have qualified for their first Finals since 1970 but they had been eliminated in the first round.

England completed their matches with a 2–1 win over Spain with a team that lined up 4-4-2, again with a mobile strike force – this time Keegan and Woodcock – and interestingly with a midfield start for Glenn Hoddle alongside Brooking, Wilkins and Terry McDermott. England left Italy with pride if not satisfaction but something had changed in the positive approach that the Greenwood reign had shown to date and over the next year, England spluttered and in truth, were fortunate to qualify for the 1982 World Cup Finals.

Part of the reason lay in the same old mistake of not playing with two wingers as England's history has shown time and time again to be their favoured approach. Part of the reason lay with a pressure that England laid on themselves with a lack of stability and certainty. Greenwood had rebuilt England's credibility with a core nucleus of players, which mixed youth with experience and with a fine balance. The logical step would have been to continue to let the players that had taken England so far to continue with little change, but Greenwood, understandably, wanted to try and few new combinations and for the opening match of the World Cup Qualifying campaign introduced Eric Gates – a talented winger from Ipswich – along with Bryan Robson and Graham Rix (Arsenal). He reintroduced the Ipswich number nine, Paul Marine to lead the attack. It was a new look side that won with ease against Norway (4–0) at Wembley. However, one has to ask whether such radical change was needed?

Did it unsettle the squad? What was Greenwood seeking that had been missing in the great victories over Spain and Argentina?

England's troubled year began with their match away to Romania – another World Cup qualifier – which they lost 2–1. The England selection again included Gates, Rix and Robson and also re-introduced Gary Birtles to play alongside Tony Woodcock. Romania has never been an easy venue to visit and one has to question whether it was right to throw four inexperienced players in what was a hostile environment?

The next qualifier was at home to Switzerland and England fielded a 4-4-2 formation with Mariner and Woodcock leading the forward line and supported by the recalled Coppell, McDermott, Brooking and Robson. England won 2–1 but it is hard to argue that England looked the same threat as they had been in either 1979 as they sailed through qualification or in the build up to 1980 Europeans.

England, over the next few months, looked unsettled and a pale imitation of themselves from 79. They drew 0–0 in the return match against Romania at Wembley. In May 1981, they then lost home matches 0–1 against Brazil and Scotland 0–1 and only managed to draw 0–0 with Wales at Wembley. What had gone wrong in just one year?

The situation then went from bad to worse with defeat to Switzerland (2–1) in Basle leaving both Greenwood pondering his resignation and England needing to win in Hungary to have a chance of qualifying for the 1982 Finals. After all the great work that Greenwood had achieved from 1977 to 1980, one has to wonder why didn't he try to naturally evolve the side rather than radically alter its structure? Maybe Greenwood was seeking a formula to take England forward another step but he not only had found it, England were in decline back to the bad days of 1976 and 77.

There could not have been more pressure on Greenwood s England took the field against Hungary but it was his protégé from his West Ham days who saved his face and played his greatest match for England. Trevor Brooking stood tall and scored twice as England won 3–1 in the home of the great Hungarian side from 1953 – a team so admired by Greenwood and which had had a profound influence on his own coaching style. Such are life's twists and ironies. It was arguably the first time England had prevailed in a "pressure" situation since the 1966. England had qualified with ease for the 1980 European Championships and had failed to qualify for any "Finals" since for the 1968 Europeans when the qualifying group was based off the Home Nations Championship but the Scots should have qualified if they had taken their chances. But they didn't and England prevailed. In fact this was one of England's best results, in a competitive international, in over a decade and this fact alone illustrates the depth of England's troubles during the 70s.

One of the missing points about Ramsey's wingless wonders is that they carried real threat from all parts of the field and especially when counterattacking. If one considers Bobby Charlton's goal against Mexico in the 1966 tournament when he ran at the heart of the Mexican defence before shooting from 30 yards – when can you recall the last England player to score such a goal? And in a competitive game?

Hurst is famed for his hat-trick in the Final. His third and final goal has been shown thousands of times on television with the immortal words "They think it is all over ... It is now!"

Who was the last striker to shoot with such power in a major match?

So often England seemed to freeze when they entered the biggest matches. Throughout the 70s and early 80s, they lacked match winners in the most pressurized of scenarios. As Bill Shankly noted at the start of this book, football is a simple game but it was made complicated as players sought to build off defensive strength rather than possessing the confidence to be direct and aggressive. England lacked aggression in the big matches and the opposition sensed it.

England just qualified for the World Cup Finals for 1982 but without much pride. After the match in Hungary, they famously lost at the start of the 81–82 season in Norway (2–1) which is most famed for the Norwegian Commentator's excitement at the victory:

> *"Lord Nelson, Lord Beaverbrook, Sir Winston Churchill, Sir Anthony Eden, Clement Attlee, Henry Cooper, Lady Diana ... we have beaten them all, we have beaten them all. Maggie Thatcher, can you hear me? Maggie Thatcher ... your boys took a hell of a beating! Your boys took a hell of a beating!"*[63]
> **Bjorge Lillelien**

England sealed qualification with a 1–0 home Victory over Hungary but it did appear that Greenwood had been hurt and affected by England's step backwards during 1980-81. Greenwood prepared England thoroughly for the 82 Finals and England performed with honour, leaving the tournament undefeated but one always wonders what could have been. The team that took the field was solid and balanced but arguably lost the match-winning player from midfield that could unlock the best. The team for the Finals was:

Shilton, Mills (Captain), Sansom, Butcher, Thompson,
Coppell, Robson, Wilkins, Rix, Mariner, Francis

The team was compact and able but how many players could really do the unpredictable, which was needed against the very best? Was there a case for including Hoddle or Cunningham in the team to bring the extra touch of creativity? Or even a midfield general such as Dennis Mortimer who had helped Aston Villa win the Championship in 1981? Aston Villa won the league in 1981 and went on to win the 1982 European Cup, but not one of their players stood in the above team.

---

63   http://en.wikipedia.org/wiki/Bj%C3%B8rge_Lillelien - cite_note-3#cite_note-3 (Bjorge Lillelien) [accessed: October 2014].

In fairness, Greenwood was unfortunate not to have the services of either Brooking or Keegan until the final match versus Spain. It is fair to argue that both were world-class players that could have made a difference, if fully fit, when England played their second stage matches against West Germany and Spain – both of which were drawn 0–0. England were still not strong enough to be able to lose two players of their calibre.

England left Spain with honour. Greenwood had returned England to the highest levels and retired as England Manager to be succeeded by Bobby Robson. But one wonders what could have been if Greenwood had not lost faith with the class of 1979–80 and given them the chance to learn and evolve for just a further two years. The International game is very different to the domestic club scene and it takes players time to adjust and find their feet. Too often England never allowed the players the time to develop at this level. Ray Kennedy, who has been mentioned a few times during this text, only played 17 games for England between 1976 and 1980, before he made the decision to retire from England duty. Peter Barnes who did play a very important central role in England's revival only played 22 times for England, with his last game in 1982 at the age of just 25. Eric Gates, who was brought in so surprisingly in 1980, only ever played the two games for England – both World Cup qualifiers. Why was he not given any time to develop in friendly matches if he was good enough to play in a competitive match?

It was the same old story that had plagued England's progress since Ramsey. Ramsey may have been too loyal but his structure was clear and stable. The players knew where they stood and what was expected of them. One of England's failures since Ramsey was simply not developing players from the domestic game to the international game. It was a philosophy of "sink or swim" and that was never going to be good enough to build a team to be able to win International tournaments.

Three English Clubs – Nottingham Forest (79, 80), Liverpool (81) and Aston Villa (82) and won Europe's most prestigious competition and this included a whole number of players that had shown that could play with Europe's best but were not close to the England whilst Robson, Wilkins, Rix, Coppell and others seemed irreplaceable, even though England's performances in 1981–82 were not as strong as hoped. Players left in the cold included:

- Jimmy Case who had been at the heart of Liverpool's success since 1976 and yet never won a single cap. He was a traditional strong English midfield player with a shot that was one of the hardest in the game. He was, In european competition, far more experienced that Bryan Robson. Few would argue Case was the better player but he could have brought something extra to the set up and been a good understudy to the established midfield.

- Alan Kennedy, Liverpool's left-back, who scored the winning goal versus Real Madrid in Paris 1981.
- Sammy Lee, the young emerging Liverpool player that would break into the England team under Robson in 1983.
- Dennis Mortimer, Aston Villa's general.
- Gordon Cowans, Villa's creative player with the vision for the telling pass.
- Kenny Swain, Villa's capable defender.
- Gary Shaw, the young pin up boy of 1981/
- Colin Gibson, the young left midfield player that would move to Manchester United in the mid 80s.
- Tony Morley, Villa's flying wing.

The above does represent a lot of proven talent that had competed at the top of the domestic game that could not break into the English set up.

Of course, the counter argument is "were they any better than those in the team and squad?" but that is not the question. The real debate is what could have been if this pool of talent had been properly nurtured and developed by the national set up. As always, England possessed the talent but failed to have a structure that developed players for the international field.

If Robson and Wilkins had driven Manchester United to european glory as Mortimer and Cowans achieved just a few weeks prior to the World Cup, they would have been feted and any exclusion from the England team would have been unthinkable. If top-level sport is about confidence and mind-set, imagine how strong Mortimer and Cowans would have felt leading in the 82 World Cup.

Of course selection is a choice of the manager but the facts do suggest the process was less than perfect. What had Robson achieved by 1982 to be the engine and leader of England's midfield? Less than Hoddle, or Mortimer. Within a year, Robson was England's natural leader and arguably it was Wilkins who could have been dispensable, but didn't England need for creative spark in their centre?

In fairness to Greenwood, he had led England back to respectability and England's performances were far better, stronger and more consistent than they had been in 1981. Greenwood had clearly left the 1980 Europeans knowing that he needed to evolve the team, but his experiments and plans did not go as hoped. However, he developed a strong base from which could evolve. Robson, Wilkins, Rix, Sansom, were all still relatively young. However, as the depth had not been nurtured, England struggled to find consistency – especially with the frequent injuries that would beset every England manager.

England failed to qualify for the 1984 Europeans but Robson did build a new team for 86. But it was a painful journey that would continue for a long time to come. Even after the success of 1990, England would decline again in the early 90s under another good club manager. It took another who stood beyond club football in Terry Venables to revitalize a broken team into one of England's most exciting in 96. Venables had been one of England's brightest and most innovative managers with QPR before he shocked many by being appointed manager of Barcelona, winning the Spanish League and then taking them to the European Cup Final. As a result, Venables had the players' admiration and respect. Like Mercer, he could talk the players' language and they loved him in return. The result was for all to see in how England played in 96. However, a mixture of internal politics and legal distractions saw Venables unable to continue his building of England and Glenn Hoddle took over after Euro 96.

The lessons had to be learnt if England were ever going to succeed.

"I was bored as England played both West Germany and Spain in 82. If I was bored, it was bloody obvious we were not going to progress. England normally start poorly and get better in a tournament. In 82, they did the opposite. They start brilliantly by thrashing France and then gradually got worse. The managed to beat Kuwait by a single goal and then played with no energy when it mattered. It was as though they said to themselves. 'we have done enough to go home unashamed but can't be bothered to try and win the bloody thing.'"

Alan.[64]

14.

THIS IS ENGLAND - GOOD AND BAD

The 1970s was a captivating decade full of drama and subplots. It was far from perfect but it was exciting. It brought despair and anguish on the international field but England's club sides enjoyed a golden age and were one of the dominant forces in Europe. It was clear though that club football was not the best preparation for the international arena and that the overall structure of the professional game was simply not good enough.

So often over the last forty years, it has been stated that England needed to improve grassroots coaching, but England produced the players; they just didn't nurture them, once professionals, for a different game, which international soccer was. It required a different approach, mind-set and technical skill set but there is little put in place to support the development of players to the highest level.

The debate over the use of wingers was well debated in every pub during the 70s. History will say that England have played their best when playing with wingers. Ramsey's wingless wonders are the exception to the rule but relied on five of England's greatest ever players. Without the five, England were not as potent a force.

Football fans have always enjoyed lists – lists of the greatest players, their favourite all time teams and players; so the following are lists from the 1970s. They are of course, just opinions, but hopefully thought provoking.

THE VILLAINS

In simple terms, the structure of the game was simply not good enough to prepare and develop players for the international arena. The international set up relied on each individual player's own skill set and ability to adapt at speed. It is the main reason why so many very good players had such short international careers. It was a sink or swim mentality and not enough thought or planning went into what was required.

Who is to blame? It is easy to point towards the FA but most were administrators rather than footballer professionals. Everyone in the profession caries a responsibility to evolve the profession. Maybe more genuine experts were needed at the board level of the FA? Maybe the England managers needed to impose a greater structure into the international set up. Many of the managers would note how different it was to club football, but the need was to impose a better structure than was similar to ones within clubs – so maybe more "B Internationals" or trips to experience contrasting international environments to broaden the mind-set and find new experiences. All in the game appeared too caught up in the strength of the English game rather than seeking to learn from other environments.

Was it arrogance? Partly. It was probably more the "islander" mentality the English can possess at times to their downfall. The English were a dominant force in the 30s and 40s as the game was still early in its maturity. Between 1950 and 1970, the game across the world evolved and matured at a greater speed than what was taking place in England. One could not fault the passion and desire within the English game, but both the South Americans and Europeans were developing new technical aspects to the game, which were more advanced than in England.

However, England still should have been a top eight team throughout the 1970s. The fault for that does lie with the England managers, as much as the structure of the game. The tactics at times were too narrow and did not evolve, there was too much pressure carried by too few and emerging players were not prepared as was needed.

The English game needed to evolve. It needed to listen and learn far better than it did.

THE HEROES OF THE 70S

Those that left the stage

Bobby Moore – England's captain for their World Cup triumph. His final games may have had moments of error but he was one of England's greatest ever players and at his peak in 1970.

Martin Peters – As with Moore, Peters was one of England's best players in the era and arguably he could have played for England for a couple more years. However, the team that he been such a pivotal players with was evolving and changing and it was natural that Peter's time would draw to a close.

Alan Ball – One of the heroes of 66 but also the captain under Revie for a short but successful period. It was during this period that it looked as though England were rebuilding successfully. Ball needed more time as captain.

Gordon Banks – England's greatest goalkeeper who was injured in a car crash and lost the sight of one of his eyes. England relied heavily

on Banks and he alone could have been the difference between qualifications or not for the 74 Finals

The Greats of the 70s

Ray Clemence – England were fortunate to possess two world-class
goalkeepers who rarely let England down.

Peter Shilton – as with Clemence, Shilton was world-class.

Kevin Keegan – Keegan's star of the 1970s.

Trevor Brooking – Trevor Brooking was at the heart of England's
revival under Greenwood and was the key fulcrum in attack with
Keegan. His performance in Budapest in 81 saved England from
another failure in qualifying for a World Cup.

The Unlucky

Brian Clough – should he have managed England?

Gerry Francis – Injury seemed to rob Francis of a great England
career as captain.

Dennis Mortimer – should he have been given an opportunity?

Jimmy Case – Should he have been given an opportunity?

Colin Bell – the natural successor to Charlton but sadly his career
was cut short.

Will History Remember?

Allan Clarke – one of England's most natural and talented goalscorers.

Martin Chivers – as with Clarke, a genuinely natural talent that needed nurturing.

Tony Currie – one of England's young talents in the early 70s.

Norman Hunter – one of the great defensive stalwarts of the 70s

They Could have had Longer England Careers

Tony Woodcock, Peter Barnes, Rodney Marsh, Alan Hudson, Malcolm Macdonald, Roy McFarland, David Nish, Frank Worthington, Keith Weller, Ray Kennedy, Stan Bowles

They made the most of their talent

Mick Mills, Bob Latchford, Dave Watson, Trevor Cherry, Emlyn Hughes, Mick Channon, Steve Coppell

"Consider for a moment what it means to represent one's country. England fans lived their lives through the players, so it really upsets me when a player thinks it just about them".

Colin.[65]

15.

Through Memory's Eyes
- The Views of Supporters

The interesting dimension that is often overlooked was how the supporters felt – especially the young, football mad fans of the era. As part of the research for this book, their views and memories – 40 years were on – were sought and recoded via a number of informal group sessions – retrospective focus groups. Their comments has been polished, the swearwords removed, but the words have stayed true to the comments. Each person's anonymity was promised as part of the overall process as the objective was for open comments to understand the perspective of those that supported the game in that era.

ENGLAND V POLAND

"Seems so silly now but I remember crying in the last ten minutes of the England match against Poland. I knew that we were seeing the end of our time of glory as a football nation and I was 14. I believed in England. I dreamed of playing for England and we were no longer in the World Cup. Yes it hurt."
Bill

"That 1973 team was so good and could have torn apart sides in the 74 World Cup. It was one match – one match that we did not win and suddenly it was all change. Typically English. Heroes and Villains. We build up our heroes and then trash them. Was Chivers ever the same again? No. Peters? No."
Daniel

"If one knew nothing about the bigger picture and just watched that game – then you would say that it was England that would be the third placed team in West Germany 74. We thrashed the Poles that night in every respect bar the one important one – goals.

Sounds strange but watching Emlyn Hughes walk off in tears and Norman Hunter look as though his world had caved in made me feel better. It told me they cared as much as I did. I could take defeat. I just couldn't bear it if we hadn't tried. We did, we lost, Fair play to Poland."

Tom

"The Poland match wasn't the low point – that came the next month against Italy. We just didn't compete and that was the end of Ramsey and Moore. Ramsey tried to bring new players in after that but it was too late.

Ramsey and Moore were the villains of the piece in 73. They had been the heroes of 66 and 70 and now they were seen to be past it. And those who judged these men were armchair administrators who achieved very little when it mattered. If one gets the armchair expert to be the decision-maker then guess what will happen? And it did.

Surely football shall be led by those who have been there and done it – those who know what it means to play for England. Not a man with wealth or an administrator with a paunch?"

Richard

"The Polish match was just one of those games when all goes against you. But England the truth was that England had become a poor team. Who remembers what Ramsey did after the Poland match? Everyone goes on about how badly Ramsey was treated but he basically jettisoned most of the players and in his last game he choose a whole number of new players such as a Phil Parkes, Trevor Brooking, Mike Pejic, Stan Bowles, Martin Dobson, and Dave Watson. I think these were all new caps. Which of these players were better than the younger players in the Poland match – Shilton, Tony Currie, Kevin Hector, and Martin Chivers? It was crass and panic. Ramsey had lost the plot at the end. Yes Brooking went on the great things but Currie should have too. Watson became a regular but he was not as good as either McFarland or Hunter. All this showed was that England had great depth of talent and players that were around the same level. But where was the plan and thinking?"

John

"I sulked for days afterwards until my sister came up and said, "Are you some kind of wimp who can't see England lose? That did the trick."

Andy

ENGLAND WITH SIR ALF, BOBBY AND MARTIN

"I recall everyone saying that the football under Joe Mercer was so much better than under Ramsey. Was that true? Mercer changed a couple of players and brought in Worthington, Weller and Keegan but this was just superficial. The only change was personnel. Ramsey was the best England manager ever. He knew what he was doing and the FA just reacted badly. We just went from bad to worse from then on over the next five years until Greenwood got us excited again with two wingers in Barnes and Coppell and started to attack again. We might lose but at least we were going for it."

Adam

"I often wonder what team England would have had for the 78 World Cup if Ramsey had stayed in charge and here is a guess: Parkes – Madeley, Hughes, Watson, McFarland – Currie, Brooking, Bell or Francis, Channon – Keegan, Macdonald. They would have had the potential to play against anyone. How does that compare to Revie's team? I mean do you remember Mike Doyle, Trevor Cherry, Stuart Pearson – good guys but not internationals. Ramsey knew a good player who could handle the international arena. Revie resorted to his trusted type. Ramsey could have taken England into a great new era and Francis would have been Ramsey's type of player."

Nick

"I never understood why Sir Alf spoke like a Tory MP. This was a man from Dagenham. Why did he have to learn to speak differently in order to get on?"

John

"I always wondered whether the politics in the game defeated England before they set foot on the pitch. The best players were not always picked. And what happened with Bobby Moore? Why was he never knighted? Why did football not laud him? I guess because he upset someone somewhere.

We have Sir Bobby Charlton – rightly so. We have Sir Geoff Hurst. Did he deserve it more than Bobby Moore? Moore was our figurehead. Hurst was a great player but not as good as either Moore or Peters. They too should have been knighted. But I also wondered if the England set up turned its back on Peters soon after because of the failure in 73? Moore and Peters would be in the all time England squad. Hurst would struggle. But yes he did score the hat trick to win the cup."

    Bob

"It is hard to look back. I remember meeting Martin Peters. They man just left me dazed with his presence. Then Bobby Moore joined him and I thought I was in the presence of gods. These guys made me and England proud. How do we repay them for giving us something so great? I won't hear a word against them. To me they were England and when they played I believed we could win against anyone. Fast-forward seven years and I was at Wembley as England were made to look like a Third Division team against the Dutch. How had we fallen so low so fast?"

    Charlie

"Moore – what a man. He had the common touch and made everyone feel better about themselves. The man was a legend.

    Ian

"I went to see Jimmy Greaves testimonial in 1972 between Spurs and Feyenoord. I think Spurs won 2–1. There were 45,000 there at White Hart Lane. Martin Peters looked like a man that knew he was world-class that night. He looked full of confidence and I remember thinking, "that man has come into his own and will be go onto great things". It did not surprise him when he scored four in one game against Manchester United. It did shock me when England dropped him."

Adrian

"I was a Norwich City fan and when Martin Peters joined us I thought, "That's it, we are now a serious club."

Charles

ENGLAND IN THE 1970S

"I know that the 70s weren't the best period but I did love the way English teams would run at the opposition. Charlton led the way with his direct powerful running and shoots. Bell was a great second in this and he should be better remembered. Then there was Francis, Channon, Keegan. Great direct players that would challenge the opposition. That was English football. We would say, "we may not be as good as you but we will take you on and we give our best." Brilliant. The problem was that our best was not always good enough."

Bryan

"I loved England as we played direct attacking football with intent whilst the Europeans played with great skill but no passion. The problem was that they kept winning. But there was no excitement in them. They were skilful but cold. No wonder players loved it when they came to play in England and could feel the atmospheres in the grounds. Whatever was good or bad about England, the fans made it special."

Bryan

"I reckon it was Clive Woodward who taught other sports how to think and plan to become competitive at the world stage. The cycling and rowing followed and nowadays there is real professionalism and planning in how the international teams prepare. But this is thirty years after the Dutch, Germans and Italians all had worked it out. The FA were just plain arrogant and did not understand what was needed. You can analyse it all as much as you would like, but the plain truth is that we did not have any real framework to allow for success. The England players would play on a Saturday and come together on Sunday evening to play on Wednesday – so two days real preparation. Everyone would laugh today at such nonsense."

Paul

"Here is a thought. If the Russian linesman had ruled out Hurst's goal in 66 and the Germans had gone onto win the 66 World Cup. How would Moore and Ramsey been viewed? Of course that's the fine line of sport. But if one remembers, when England lost in Czechoslovakia, Keegan had a goal wrongly ruled offside. England would have drawn 2–2 and qualified for the 76 Europeans. Czechoslovakia won that tournament. England could have and Revie would have been seen to be a great manager. Yes England had a rough time. We had our luck in the 60s. It went against us the 70s and we over reacted. Revie was actually a good football man. Just unlucky but as Napoleon said, "surround me with lucky generals".

Alan

"I always wonder if the real problem lay in English expectations – not from the fans and not even from the press who are the ones that always get singled out, but from the directors of the game who seem to believe that England should do well by right. I suspect the players knew the truth. They knew that other teams were better prepared and organised for international matches and that we had to rely only on our talent. I reckon the players lacked confidence in international matches that they had naturally in club games. In the summer tours, England often would play well. I think of the Bicentennial Cup in the US in 76 when England played well against Brazil and Italy. Gerry Francis was captain. Wilkins made his debut against Italy. We lost to a late Brazilian goal in something like the 89th minute. Italy we beat from 2–0 down. Great spirit. These were the future and it was promising but we just could not maintain our play and why when others could? I reckon because we just lacked confidence in the management and this is beyond Ramsey and Revie. They were just the scapegoats."

Ken

"No one will ever tell me it was not a great era in football. It was fantastic in many ways and the players were crowd pleasers. They were a new breed of mavericks and rebels from the days of the 50s and 60s. Television was taking off. There was much more coverage of the game and football was very, very popular. It was the start of the modern game. The traditional game died with the 66 World Cup. The 1970 World Cup raised the bar to a whole new level. Brazil of 70 would have easily beaten England of 66 and the 74 World Cup showed new talents in the Dutch, and the Poles. 78 was all about the emergence of Argentina with Mario Kempes, Ossie Ardiles and Ricky Villa. England were still playing the same way as in 66. The world had moved on and the English club players had too. There really was not too much to complain about. Best football of my life. It was honest and true but like these players today who are paid £100,000 a week to kick a ball and fall over as soon as someone touches them. Can you remember the 1972 Cup Final when Norman Hunter helped carry the injured Mick Jones up the Wembley steps to collect his medals? That was real man, real football. That wouldn't happen today. But the today teams are not English in character but international."

Bryan

"England had so much talent in their ranks. In 1974, they could have had two teams that were better than the team that played Poland and should have been in both the 74 and 78 World Cups. We didn't because the wrong players were selected. Yes it is a moan and because we were left the disappointed ones."

Tommy

"England should have kept with Joe Mercer. He was not the most eloquent of men but he was a real football man. He also understood the big clubs and small clubs. He was popular and he had years of experience. Better still if he then taken Malcolm Allison into the England set up, we would have been one formidable coaching set up."

Joe

"Scotland were the better team in the 70s. It was their golden era. England versus Scotland games were just great games to watch. The Scots were happy as long as they beat England. Sod the rest of the world. England was all-important and in the 70s they enjoyed their moments – Dalglish scoring as Clemence let the ball through his legs or the 2–1 win at Wembley which saw their fans tear up the pitch and goals. The England team was as good as dead. They were struggling to be anything of importance."

Ken

THE APPOINTMENT OF DON REVIE

"I can remember the summer of 74 vividly. It was like the end of my youth. A new James Bond was out and was playing for laughs with Roger Moore and England appointed the manager from the hardnosed Leeds United. Both were huge disappointments."

Terry

"I was happy as he was the best manager in England."

Jack

"I bet many have said it, but Clough would have changed things completely after Ramsey and would have been a breath of fresh air. England had lost their way and needed something radical. Clough was radical. He was self-opinionated, egotistical but he knew his football and he was a winner. England would have played better football than under Revie and at the very worst; it would have been more engaging watch him take on the world's best. Clough believed he was as good as anyone and he would have raised his behaviour and game so that he would not look foolish. Clough was a very clever man and he would never have allowed himself to have looked out of his depth. I think Revie just gave up after the second year and couldn't wait to get out. Clough would never have thought as Revie did. Clough would have worked hard to find the right combinations. Revie's team started well and got worse. Clough's would have improved."

Dave

"The biggest problem with Revie was that he was so hard to like. As England manager you know it isn't going to go to plan and you are right there to be shot at. The only defence you have is whether people like you or not. Venables people liked. Everyone knew his weaknesses in business but fans liked him for his football. People liked Erickson, so his affair with the Swedish girl was overlooked. You just felt sorry for Taylor and McLaren, but they made you cringe. Robson you just had to like as he was a real footballing man – and that is what fans want to see – a man with passion and who speaks from the heart. You always knew that Robson loved his football and when *The Sun* went on the attack, most people wanted Robson to succeed which he did. I still remember the great summer of 1990 when we dreamed once again – maybe for the first time since the days of Bobby Moore."

Richard

"I can think of quite a few managers that would have been good appointments. Why? Because Leeds united split everyone's opinion and England needed someone who unite a nation – not divide it. Who would have been better? How about Bertie Mee or Ron Greenwood (in 74) or Brian Clough or Malcolm Allison or even Bill Shankly who retired at the start of the 74–75 season."

Colin

ENGLISH CLUB FOOTBALL IN THE 70S

"Everyone kept going on about how we were technically inferior but the real difference was that English football was so intense and competitive. I always think back fondly on the 70s when people like Chopper Harris would want to almost take out any attacker that was a threat. So would Jack Charlton. And Storey and Hunter. The list goes on. Attackers would not pass. It was real Alpha male "physicality. Sod technique. This was about winning."

Jon

"Unless you were there, it is impossible to understand what English football was like. It was aggressive. It was tense. As a fan, you knew it could be violent. It was where the thug resided. It was where the tribe came together. And I was just a silly young man on the side. I remember taking a beautiful girlfriend to a match and wow … it was best and worst thing I could have done. I remember getting on the tube and regretting seeing my girl surrounded by these men that looked like they could eat me for breakfast. I remember standing on the terraces and wincing at all the vulgarity … but afterwards, she was buzzing. She loved it and she loved me that day."

Jerry

"The 1970s was the era of the maverick and we loved them. There was Frank Worthington with his long flowing hair and moustache, which looked like he had come off the set of a Western. There was Stan Bowles, Rodney Marsh, Charlie George and of course the great George Best. They lived hard and played hard. They didn't care about anything but football, girls and drink. And we loved them."

Peter

"The players of the 70s were every bit as good as those of the 50s and 60s. In fact maybe better. The problem was that other countries had become savvier at dealing with us. If one looks at the Leeds – Bayern Munich European Cup Final of 1975, Leeds were the better team by far and had a goal wrongly ruled out for offside and a penalty denied when Clarke was taken down by Beckenbauer. Leeds dominated that match and should have been European Champions, but they lost to a sucker punch. It was Ali v Foreman and Munich were Ali. But Munich were scared of Leeds. It was the same with England. We were a threat but we lost to silly goals and naive play."

Alex

"I remember the arguments in my house between my brother and father over systems. Everything was about the defensive system. My father would go on and on about Stanley Matthews and Tom Finney. I am sure they were great players but it was all such rubbish. Football was simply get more technically evolved and for some weird reason, the English just ignored it. We were arrogant for years until defeat after defeat made us a little bit more humble. We would believe that English football was still the best in the world even though we could never qualify for international tournaments. Being good was about winning when it mattered. The English believed their own PR."

   Donald

"I don't really care. It happened. I loved supporting Arsenal. We had a team of few great players but we were a team. We would fight to the end. We were hated but we were the Arsenal and that was all that mattered."

   Peter

"It was all so intense. Football was so important. FA Cup Final day was the day we would all come together and dream. It was glamorous, exciting, and dramatic. What moments – Keegan versus Newcastle in 74, which set him up as a true star. Moore versus his beloved West Ham in 75. Charlie Georges' winner in 71. Clarkes' diving header in 72. This was the age of heroes. England came second."

   Danny

"It was often said that the skilful players were not allowed to pay in the 70s. Not true. They were there led by Bobby Moore, George Best, Peters – but there were also a lot of great defenders that were just tough bastards. Leeds epitomised that, which is why they were hated. Leeds reflected the best and worst of England and then what do the FA do? Appoint Revie as manager. Oh goody."

Adam

"There was a big difference between league football and international. It was not joined up and the better the English league was, the worse the England team would do. If one looks at all the best countries around the world, their leagues are dominated by a few big names clubs – Real Madrid, Barcelona, Bayern Munich, Juventus, A C Milan, Ajax. These were the big name clubs. England has big name clubs too such as Liverpool, Leeds but they did not have teams that were miles better. I was a Stoke City fan and in the mid 70s, little Stoke began to attract big name players such as Geoff Hurst, Peter Shilton, Alan Hudson, plus had a real team. I remember not just how we won the League Cup against glamour boys Chelsea, but how we went head to head with mighty Arsenal in the FA Cup and how we beat mighty Leeds United in 74 and how we even topped the league table in 75. How could unglamorous Stoke achieve such things? Because English football was not what it is today and all about wealth. It was then about the glory too and basic teamwork. Stoke could have won the Championship in 75. Imagine that? Mad, well look at what Clough did at Nottingham Forest and they went on to buy Britain's first million pound footballer and win two European Cups. That was what so great about English football – it allowed your local team to compete, but it did not help the international team. There was no soul or foundation to England bar a talented group of individuals who may have been proud to play for England, but would be competing against their fellow player again a week later."

Robin

"The 70s have always been seen as a cynical time and yet so much of it has lasted the test of time – Abba, Rod Stewart, Eric Clapton and the football stars of the day such as Keegan, Brooking, Shilton, Wilkins. It was a great era."

Brian

"I went to boarding school in Norfolk and I was the only non Norwich fan there. It was as though I was a traitor and I did not even live in Norfolk. It was the local team and that was the team you were supposed to support. It was little wonder that football violence took off, as the 70s were about being free to express yourself and hell, the workingman expressed himself. The economy was terrible and football and drink was the escape route. Of course the violence was awful but it made the football even more intense and the rivalries between teams even more fierce. And then the England manager is asked to build a team that can compete with the best in the world. Yeap, that was Mission Impossible and yet Revie's name is still like that of a traitor."

Martin

"The 70s was an era of real working class heroes. The two teams I liked were Sheffield United, because Tony Currie was immense and I liked QPR who could have won the Championship under Gerry Francis in 75–76. Francis would just directly attack teams whilst Currie could have been a George

Best. Both should have been world-class players that had the glory. But neither quite lived up to their potential through injury and bad management. English football had the players. They had real working class heroes that their fan on the terrace adored. Where it all went wrong was in the boardrooms and behind the scenes. The administrators were just glory boys with no pedigree."

Geoffrey

"How good was football in the 70s? Well I remember a competition called the Watney Cup, which was pre-season and *Match of the Day* covered it and it drew in four million viewers for an irrelevant cup. Football was not just good. It was important."

Jack

"The best way of telling you about football then was by asking this question. In the season after the World Cup, which team was top of the League after August? Forget the Gerd Mullers, Johan Cruyffs, Dino Zoffs – little Carlisle United topped the league. They beat Chelsea at Stamford Bridge in the first match of the season 2–0. Their winger was a chap called Chris Balderstone who went on to play cricket for England. He played football in the winter. Cricket in the summer. What a life eh? English football was full of romantic stories. In no other part of the world, could that have happened?"

Chris

"English football is about club football first. England came second. I recall watching TV programmes like *Man about the House* and *Minder* and they used to support Fulham. I couldn't get my head around it, as Fulham were pretty poor. But then someone explained it to me – the fun of supporting a team was the hope for glory and that half the team would be truly bad. But supporting a team is like a relationship – there is good and bad, but it is the promise of something amazing that makes it worthwhile. You may go through years of frustration but then a single moment can make it all worthwhile. That is what supporting a team is all about. It is easy to support the team at the top of the table. In the 70s, fans would support Stoke City, West Ham, Leicester City, Nottingham Forest, even Fulham – and we had a dream."

Terry

"What were the 70s like? The sporting arena was about brutal contests – Ali–Frazier. Leeds–Liverpool. Celtic–Rangers. England–Australia with Lillee and Thommo targeting English bodies in Cricket. That was sport we loved and England lacked that spark in football."

Tony

"I remember going to my first football match. I stood on the stands and heard women say words I could hardly believe. The men were full of aggression and anger. No wonder the players played as hard as they could. One mistake and they would have 30,000 people singing "wanker" about them. The players played hard as a result."

Stuart

BIBLIOGRAPHY:

Bill Shankly. (2014) *Own Words*. [Online] Available from: http://www.shankly.com/article/2517 [Accessed: 21 October 2014].

Daily Mail. (2009) *Bill Shankly: The top 10 quotes of a Liverpool legend 50 years to the day since he took over*. [Online] Available from: http://www.dailymail.co.uk/sport/football/article-1232318/Bill-Shankly-The-quotes-Liverpool-legend-50-years-day-took-over.html [Accessed: 1 September 2014].

The Guardian. (2008) *Is English football really the best in Europe?* [Online] Available from: http://www.theguardian.com/football/2008/apr/01/europeanfootball.sport1 [Accessed: 21 November 2014].

This Day in Football History. (2010) *14 May 1938 – Hapgood Had The Right Idea*. [Online] Available from: http://tdifh.blogspot.co.uk/2010/05/14-may-1938-hapgood-had-right-idea.html [Accessed: 10 November 2014].

Spartacus Educational. (2014) *West Ham United Biographies: Len Goulden*. [Online] Available from: http://spartacus-educational.com/WHgouldenL.htm [Accessed: 21 November 2014].

BBC Sport. (2010) *Defeat by US still hurts, says England old boy Williams*. [Online] Available from: http://news.bbc.co.uk/sport1/hi/football/world_cup_2010/8728535.stm [Accessed: 22 October 2014].

The Guardian. (2010) *5 June 1968: Ramsey pays for England's first ever red card.* [Online] Available from: http://www.theguardian.com/sport/2009/jun/06/england-first-red-card-mullery [Accessed: 21 November 2014].

The Guardian. (2005) *Semi-final or bust for Sven, pay-off permitting.* [Online] Available from: http://www.theguardian.com/football/2005/oct/08/sport.comment3 [Accessed: 28 August 2014].

McIlvanney, H. (1973) *England shown the way out. The Guardian.* [Online] 2011. Available from: http://observer.theguardian.com/englandfootball/story/0,9565,541541,00.html [Accessed: 11 October 2014].

Briggs, S. (2008) *England v Germany at the Olympic Stadium: The Berlin Effect. The Telegraph.* [Online] 18 November 2008. Available from: http://www.telegraph.co.uk/sport/football/teams/england/3479037/England-v-Germany-at-the-Olympic-Stadium-The-Berlin-Effect-Football.html [Accessed: 2 August 2014].

Eurosport. (2012) *Tomaszewski exclusive: England 'miracle' in 1973 like beating Bolsheviks.* [Online] Available from:

http://au.eurosport.com/football/world-cup/2018/england-v-poland-classic-matches_sto3459419/story.shtml [Accessed: 23 September 2014].

Channel 4. (2013) England v Poland at Wembley – ITN archive (1973). [Online] Available from: http://www.channel4.com/news/poland-england-wembley-world-cup-1973-tomaszewski [Accessed: 19 November 2014].

Daily Star. (2013) *Martin Peters warns England: Don't blow it like we did!* [Online] Available from: http://www.dailystar.co.uk/sport/football/345141/Martin-Peters-warns-England-Don-t-blow-it-like-we-did [Accessed: 3 September 2014].

The Telegraph. (2013) *England v Poland: We murdered them in 1973 but they went to the World Cup* [Online] Available from: http://www.telegraph.co.uk/sport/football/teams/england/10375969/England-v-Poland-We-murdered-them-in-1973-but-they-went-to-the-World-Cup.html [Accessed: 21 November 2014].

Daily Mail. (2013) *Shilton, Hunter and Clarke share their memories of England's 1973 World Cup qualification heartbreak* [Online] Available from: http://www.dailymail.co.uk/sport/football/article-2458091/England-v-Poland-1973-Peter-Shilton-Norman-Hunter-Allan-Clarkes-memories-heartbreak.html [Accessed: 6 November 2014].

Daily Mirror. (2013) *Poland's other 1973 hero Jan Domarski back to give England the spooks* [Online] Available from: http://www.mirror.co.uk/sport/football/england-v-poland-polands-1973-2368049 [Accessed: 29 July 2014].

Redknapp, H. (ed.) (2013) *Always Managing: My Autobiography.* London: Edbury Press.

Daily Mail. (2012) *Jeff Powell: Sat alongside 99 schoolkids, Bobby Moore's dignified celebration of his 100 caps.* [Online] Available from: http://www.dailymail.co.uk/sport/football/article-2215262/Bobby-Moore-reached-100-caps-dignified-way-sharp-contrast-Ashley-Cole.html [Accessed: 7 November 2014].

The Guardian. (2009) *Hero cast aside – Sir Alf Ramsey, 1970s.* [Online] Available from: http://www.theguardian.com/football/2009/may/21/seven-deadly-sins-football-alf-ramsey-england [Accessed: 21 November 2014].

Daily Mirror. (2012) *Sir Alf axe STILL hurts: Allan Clarke on the loss that lead to World Cup hero's sacking.* [Online] Available from: http://www.mirror.co.uk/sport/football/news/england-football-team-allan-clarke-1380243 [Accessed: 1 November 2014].

The Guardian. (2012) *The forgotten story of … England under Joe Mercer.* [Online] Available from: http://www.theguardian.com/sport/blog/2012/oct/11/forgotten-story-joe-mercer-england-manager [Accessed: 30 October 2014].

Daily Mail. (2012) *The night Total Football conquered Wembley thanks to Cruyff and his Orange masters.* [Online] Available from: http://www.dailymail.co.uk/sport/football/article-2107856/England-v-Holland-Remember-1977-Total-Football-conquered-Wembley.html [Accessed: 21 November 2014].

The Mighty Mighty Whites. (2014) *Don Revie - Part 8 Disgrace and despair (1977-89).* [Online] Available from: http://www.mightyleeds.co.uk/managers/revie8.htm [Accessed: 21 November 2014].

ND - #0197 - 270225 - C0 - 234/156/12 - PB - 9781780913643 - Gloss Lamination